10/15 LN

Making

A Social Skills Program for Inclusive Settings

Ruth Herron Ross
Beth Roberts-Pacchione

SECOND EDITION

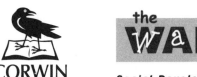

CORWIN
A SAGE Company

the WANNA PLAY program
Social Development and Behavior Management

CORWIN
A SAGE Company

FOR INFORMATION:

Corwin
A SAGE Company
2455 Teller Road
Thousand Oaks, California 91320
(800) 233-9936
Fax: (800) 417-2466
www.corwin.com

SAGE Ltd.
1 Oliver's Yard
55 City Road
London EC1Y 1SP
United Kingdom

SAGE India Pvt. Ltd.
B 1/I 1 Mohan Cooperative
Industrial Area
Mathura Road, New Delhi 110 044
India

SAGE Asia-Pacific Pte. Ltd.
33 Pekin Street #02-01
Far East Square
Singapore 048763

Acquisitions Editor: Jessica Allan
Associate Editors: Allison Scott
Editorial Assistant: Lisa Whitney
Production Editor: Veronica Stapleton
Copy Editor: Matthew Adams
Typesetter: C&M Digitals (P) Ltd.
Proofreader: Wendy Jo Dymond
Cover Designer: Rose Storey
Permissions Editor: Karen Ehrmann

Copyright © 2011 by Corwin

Printed in the United States of America

Library of Congress Cataloging-in-Publication Data

Ross, Ruth, 1974-

Making friends, preK-3: a social skills program for inclusive settings/Ruth Herron Ross, Beth Roberts-Pacchione. — 2nd ed.

p. cm.

Rev. ed. of: Wanna play.

Includes bibliographical references and index.

ISBN 978-1-4129-8113-2 (pbk.)

1. Social skills—Study and teaching (Elementary) 2. Social skills in children—Study and teaching. 3. Children with disabilities. 4. Children with social disabilities. I. Roberts-Pacchione, Beth. II. Ross, Ruth, 1974- Wanna play. III. Title.

HM691.R67 2011

371.92'80482—dc22 2010045948

This book is printed on acid-free paper.

11 12 13 14 15 10 9 8 7 6 5 4 3 2 1

Contents

Acknowledgments

First and foremost, we wish to thank our families for the love, support, and faith in us they have shown over the years. We would like to particularly thank Ron, Sarah, Kylie, Scott, Paul, and William for their never-ending patience. We would have never gotten this far without you.

We would like to thank those involved in the Wanna Play Program's Internship Program for their energy and enthusiasm. Your work will touch many children for years to come, and we wish you luck in your future. We would also like to thank our staff for their hard work, dedication, and creativity. Without your love and genius, the program would never have grown the way it has.

Finally, we would like to thank the families we have been working with over the years. The parents and children we have had the honor to work with have taught us the true meaning of strength. We have learned more than we have taught.

Thank you,
Ruth and Beth

About the Authors

 **Ruth Herron Ross,** codirector and coauthor of the Wanna Play Program, holds a Bachelor of Science in early childhood elementary education from Beaver College and a Master of Science in special education and specialty reading from St. Joseph's University. Ruth has dedicated her life to the education of children with special needs and the autism community. Ruth has worked with children from ages 2 to 17 and is trained in a variety of one-on-one early intervention and therapeutic programs such as ABA, Floortime, Son-Rise, and Interactive Metronome. Her 15 years of education experiences, combined with her early intervention training, gave Ruth the foundation of knowledge in autism, language development, and socialization skills to create the Wanna Play Program. Over the years she has provided numerous trainings to parents and professional and is a founding member and lead trainer of the Valley Forge Education Services' community outreach program, Caring Kinships: ASD—Matching Families With Sitters. Ruth has been facilitating social skill groups and individual sessions for children as director of the Pennsylvania location for the past 10 years and in the New Jersey location for the past 2 years.

 **Beth Roberts-Pacchione** is coauthor and codirector of the Wanna Play Program. Beth received her Master of Arts degree in counseling psychology at Eastern University and is continuing the process to become a licensed counselor in Pennsylvania. After Beth's daughter was diagnosed with Global Developmental Delay and autistic tendencies, she was uncertain about how to best help her. She decided both to receive training in and administer a home-based program called Son-Rise. She also researched, tested, and utilized many different alternative therapies, dietary interventions, and behavioral approaches. Beth has also been trained in Floortime and Interactive Metronome, and she has worked in ABA programs. For the past 10 years at the Pennsylvania location of the Wanna Play Program, Beth has been facilitating social skill groups and individual sessions for children ages 3 through 17 years. She is now beginning to counsel adults to provide therapeutic support to those parents whose children have been diagnosed with special needs.

Introduction

Welcome to the Wanna Play Program

We are very thrilled for the opportunity to put together this revised edition of *Wanna Play: Friendship Skills for Preschool and Elementary Grades*. The Wanna Play Program was developed as the result of our experience in early intervention and social behavior development. Both of us have had personal journeys with the development of this program. It has been inspired by our own children's growth and that of all the children we have been lucky enough to join for a part of their journey. We found that children were not applying the social skills they had learned in school and community settings. There were few programs dealing with social-ization that accommodated children on many different interactive levels. We have directed social groups in our Pennsylvania location as well as running groups and training professionals in schools and other therapeutic environments. We began developing a meaningful approach to these skills and realized the need for this type of supportive, instructional programming. This led to the creation of Wanna Play, Inc. in 2001. The program is proud to be celebrating 10 years of providing social skills development and behavior support. Over the years, this program has been used with success by everyone from teachers to babysitters. Developing interactive social ability and an understanding of social norms in children is the responsibility of all adults and crosses disciplines.

We have reworked this edition to be more effective and added to the program's strengths for a more enriched social experience. There has been new research into the importance of social skills and the acquisition of these skills. Most children's programming includes a social and behavior element. The understanding that a child's social and behavioral development is nec-essary for the development of cognitive and physical skills is becoming more and more readily accepted in educational models. Therefore, we have strengthened the program's effectiveness in inclusive classroom settings. We have seen that when these topics are used in inclusive settings, the strategies used by adults and the behaviors and social skills taught become part of the school culture and all children benefit. We have made this edition more user-friendly for teach-ers by adding more detail to the activities themselves. There are details guiding teachers with lesson objectives and goals. More suggestions have been added for compensating for differ-ent cognitive and developmental levels. Specifics about lesson preparation and implementa-tion time have been added to help the flow of lesson planning. All of these changes will help teachers provide a strong social development program in their schools. It is very important for children to develop an emotional vocabulary to express their feelings and frustrations. Many negative behaviors come from children's inability to communicate what they want and how they feel. We have addressed this with the addition of a new chapter that helps children with understanding emotional expression. The chapter looks at emotional expression from the perspectives of (1) personal expression and (2) interpreting others' emotions when we are interacting. It is important for children to be able to not only express themselves appropriately but also understand others' feelings and respond to them in a meaningful way.

Even though the new focus is on the inclusive classroom, there is a wide audience who would benefit from utilizing this program and incorporating the lessons and activities into their work with children. Many of the activities will still work with small groups, and we have put suggestions in place to help those using the curriculum to adapt them to many models. Other educators working with children in school settings, including school psychologists and school counselors, can incorporate the curriculum by using the lessons with individual children, small groups, or classrooms. Therapy professionals whose area of specialization impacts social development, such as occupational therapists, speech therapists, and behavioral specialists, can also utilize the program and use it with their clients. Mental health professionals including psychologists, psychiatrists, or social workers can use the lessons as part of their therapy sessions that concentrate on the development of social awareness. Caregivers including parents, childcare providers, and in-home support staff who are concentrating on their children's social development can use the program, particularly those with special needs children who have home therapy programs.

Based on our experience, a child with social challenges does not learn the skills necessary for successful interaction by observing typically developing peers in the classroom. More direct instruction on how to socially interact is needed in order for them to learn these abstract skills. A child does not need to have a diagnosis in order to have challenges in developing social skills. We provide the training to teachers and professionals and instruction to children in a child-centered curriculum to encourage success in all areas of social interaction.

The underlying intention of all of the attitudinal approach strategies is to be in touch with our own positive playfulness. We need to be aware of outside influences that affect our affect. When we are working on anything as important as children's social development, the time spent working on our own attitude is as important as the time spent instructing the children. We need to make sure that the children's time is their time and that we put our own concerns aside during this time. If you are reading this curriculum, it is because you love children and want to help them. Enjoy what you are giving them, enjoy what they are giving you, and enjoy seeing the benefits of both your efforts. A universally accepted belief in education, therapy, and any developmental discipline for children is that modeling skills and behaviors is the best way for children to internalize them—therefore, we say to you, above all, *have fun*.

Guidelines for Curriculum Success

You will not be successful using this curriculum unless you read this section. This is the only time you will read a negative statement in this book. The true success of this program begins with understanding the philosophy behind the curriculum so that you can help the children to truly learn the social concepts taught. The purpose of this section is to give the facilitator an overview of the key concepts and to support him or her in understanding the importance of these concepts to enhance the child's success. In this section, we explain the different parts of each unit and how to apply the lessons.

ATTITUDE

Your *affect* has a great *effect* on the development of social behavior. The facilitator's attitude is the key to a child's ability to make the attempts necessary to inspire true interaction with adults and their peers. Children will develop the affects they observe, so we want to be mindful of what we are thinking and feeling when we are introducing social concepts. Give yourself the opportunity to observe any and all behaviors without judgment. Listening to and really seeing the child is the best way to find the keys for helping to develop social ability. We have developed this program on a child-centered model of teaching so we can choose and adapt activities and games to suit the child's interest. Remember that the child is his or her own best expert, and focus on the child's specific needs. Present suggestions and strategies so the child will see how the skill benefits her or him. Children do not develop appropriate social skills because it makes others happy. They adopt appropriate social behavior because over time they learn that those behaviors get them what they want.

A positive attitude does not mean that we need to be upbeat at all times. You can be firm and even discipline and still have a positive affect, as you will see when we discuss managing behavior later on in this section. It is more about internalizing a calm affect and having a "can do" attitude. Part of this is being nonjudgmental of the behavior that a child may choose. We do not know why a child will choose a particular behavior, and we cannot put the assumption that they are "bad" or being disrespectful. Instead, these behaviors are opportunities for us to help the child to see the benefit of choosing a positive affect like the one we have been portraying.

What we have found successful for ourselves is to check in with others about how we are feeling about a particular incident or child. If we feel overwhelmed, frustrated, or just fed up with a certain child's behavior, then it is our responsibility to re-center ourselves and find a new, proactive way of approaching the situation. Create a support system of people who focus on finding the solution and not on reliving the problem. We need to remember the mantra that there is always a solution to better help the child.

EYE CONTACT

Eye contact is an essential tool to successfully negotiate our social world. This skill is necessary in classroom settings for children to be able to develop concepts, comprehend information, and stay on topic when communicating with others. In social settings with adults and peers, eye contact skills help children to develop appropriate understanding of facial expression, reciprocal social communication, and the ability to stay calm and focused in a conflict situation.

In educational settings, the assumption that is commonly made is that eye contact is not crucial for children to learn. Children with very poor eye contact have been observed using some skills and retaining a little of the information that was introduced when they were not making eye contact. It has been our experience that without eye contact, children do not retain all the information they need for success in social and school settings, even though they retain some information on occasion.

When children with poor eye contact are interacting with adults and peers, their inability to make eye contact impacts both their development of social skills and how others perceive their social abilities. The complexity of reciprocal interaction is a combination of learned concrete skills and abstract nonverbal behaviors. Learning these two facets of social interaction requires both the learning of concrete concepts and using honed observational abilities. Without sustainable frequency and duration in eye contact, children cannot learn social concepts and are not able to observe their surroundings. This results in partially developed and poorly formed social skills. Many people misinterpret poor eye contact and make negative judgments about children with disabilities or challenges. Children are identified as guilty, aloof, or disrespectful if they have poor eye contact as they get into the later elementary ages. By concentrating on eye contact now, children will be able to represent themselves and express their needs in a positive way as they get older.

Many times we have had people point out the different ways that eye contact is used in different cultures. It is true that eye contact is used differently in different cultures and that making eye contact holds different meanings. It is important to be aware of the cultural background of the population you are working with and to develop sensitivity to their needs. However, in every culture eye contact is used as a nonverbal tool for communication in some way, either by using it or avoiding it. We are not suggesting that children be taught to make consistent, sustained eye contact as if having a staring contest with everyone they encounter. The program's objective is to help children to develop the understanding that eye contact is an important tool that is needed when interacting with others. This is an important lesson for those children who actively avoid eye contact, even when it is appropriate, due to sensory challenges, poor self-esteem, a lack of social awareness, or difficulty with focus and attention.

This is why we have dedicated an entire unit to strengthening eye contact and building the concept that sustainable eye contact is vital for successful social interaction. We also put a strong focus on the development of eye contact throughout the rest of the curriculum so children understand that it is skill that we use consistently. The earlier we make eye contact a priority in the social development of children, the more success they will have as they get older.

The unit on eye contact teaches the concepts on why and how we use eye contact. After this unit, we need to be consistent in using the following strategies to help children develop eye contact throughout all of their daily interactions. We feel the following techniques are the most effective and the easiest to implement in home and school. For overall curriculum success, utilize the suggestion listed in the Generalization and Consistency section of each lesson. These strategies should be used on a daily basis.

ASKING LEADING QUESTIONS

Leading questions are a useful teaching tool in many situations. This curriculum uses leading questions in the introduction section of each lesson. The purpose of the questions is to help the children understand the abstract concepts that will be a foundation for the activities in the lesson. Using questions and cues directs the children to formulate answers based on their own experiences. This helps the children to internalize the concept and generalize it back into a social setting. Use leading questions when developing concept maps and brainstorming lists.

Things to remember when forming your leading questions:

- Use open-ended questions, avoiding yes-or-no questions.
- Use "Wh" questions, concentrating on asking *what* and *where* questions first to help children develop concrete concepts. When asking why questions, use additional clues and specific situations to keep children on topic and encourage diverse answers.
- Use pictures and suggestions from children's immediate personal experience, especially with early readers.
- Give clues from past lessons.

LEARNING THROUGH FREE PLAY

The Wanna Play Program begins with a child-centered philosophy and offers a curriculum to teach young children that playing is fun. Playing with friends is difficult for many children for many different reasons. We teach children the positive phrases and skills necessary to be successful in play scenarios. We also believe that it is best to teach and show children these strategies while they are playing.

Facilitated free play is beneficial to children for many reasons. It allows learning to occur based on something they are interested in. Also, they can immediately see the benefit of using the strategies we are teaching. All sessions will be more successful if at least part of the time is used for facilitated free play to show children how much fun it can be to play with others if they use the skills we help them learn. There is a tendency to think that for children to be learning and developing socialization, we need to always do structured activities or worksheets. As teachers and facilitators, we want to remember that allowing children free play time lets them practice and generalize the skills they have learned in the lessons. Our role in this free play is to be active observers and facilitators so that the children are constantly in a socially supportive environment even though it is open-ended play. The key to success in this process is knowing when to stand back and observe and when to interact and facilitate.

We call the type of facilitation we use "guerilla facilitation." The facilitator stands back, actively observing the children's interactive play, looking for opportunities to prompt social language, suggest an effective play skill, and expand play themes and diversity. This active observing also allows us to keep watch for those children who choose exclusive play over interaction and to look for opportunities to redirect them toward interaction with their peers. These are the cues that teachers and facilitators should look for as opportunities to facilitate and help the children:

- Simple, exclusive, or repetitious play
- Conflict situations such as grabbing behaviors
- Inappropriate language or misused phrases

As the interactive facilitators, we need to keep aware of the intention of the free play situations. We can run the risk of "overfacilitation" during free play and thus not give the children the opportunity to try the skills we have introduced. "Overfacilitation" can happen when we are watching children attempting to use new skills on their own and we move in too soon to help. With each of the cues that we have suggested, we want to watch and see if the children self-correct or attempt a different strategy when interacting before we move in to offer new techniques.

During these free plays, the focus should also be on the interaction of the children. The introduction of a new game and the teaching of new play bring the focus onto the adult and take time away from the children's interaction. We suggest preparation time be spent before the free play to learn new games or activities and help the children prepare for the play.

ADAPTATIONS FOR AGE AND DEVELOPMENTAL LEVEL

In each of the sections, the games and activities have been used in classes from kindergarten to third grade and for a wide variety of developmental levels. Adaptations will need to be made to fit the group you are working with. The language needs to be changed, and so do some of the materials. Unfortunately, we cannot put all of these things in our book because it would be too long to publish, but what we have offered are some guidelines for making adaptations for the group you are working with.

Know your group. In most cases, people who are starting with our program will be working with a group they have some familiarity with and will have a clear knowledge of the individual students' strengths and challenges, as well as the dynamics of the group. In some cases, the group will be new students or known students in a new grouping, and the facilitator will need to figure out the dynamic. Either way, like all resources, each person working with the children needs to use the program we have laid out in the best way for his or her group of children.

MANAGING BEHAVIOR

We have already discussed the importance of a positive attitude when we work with children. It is just as important to discuss the affect and attitude of the children we are working with and how we can help them to maintain appropriate behavior. In most situations when a child is using inappropriate behaviors, there is a sensory solution that will help them to re-center and cope with the situation. Children also use learned inappropriate behaviors and need to be taught the appropriate ways to interact, seek attention, and get what they want. Children can implement many different behaviors to communicate their wants and needs. Some options they may try to use include negative behaviors such as crying, having tantrums, attempting to hurt feelings, and using emotional manipulation such as pity or guilt. We attempt to try to react the same way to all of these behaviors.

In every situation, we need to remember that the first thing that needs to be done is to wait for the child to calm down before we introduce solutions or new behaviors to the child. We suggest a consistent reaction to minimize negative behavior. Assess the situation. If it is a situation where there is a possibility of negotiation, then do it before the negative behavior begins. When a child is not getting what she or he wants, suggest different options as a second attempt such as trades, deals, and bargains like sharing and picking something new. Make deals and bargains, but hold the child to his or her part of the deal.

- **Trades**—Someone has something you want; find something they might want to trade with you.
- **Deals**—Make a deal so both people get what they want. (For example, you use it for 5 minutes, then I use it for 5 minutes.)
- **Share**—We all use it at the same time. (This involves working on waiting, asking with kind words, and taking short turns.)
- **Pick New**—Find a new cool thing to play with.

In certain situations there is no room for negotiation. Let the child know that the situation is not going to change. If the child continues to use negative behaviors, let the child know that he or she has the choice of complying now or during "their time." Be specific about what his or her time is (e.g., "You have a choice . . . you can clean your room now or after dinner at TV time. It is your choice, but your room needs to be cleaned.").

SENSORY SUPPORT

In our work we have found much success in incorporating sensory diets in the social training that we do. Many of the children we work with are also dealing with various levels of sensory integration issues, and we have found that they have a direct impact on the children's behavioral choices. Some of the techniques we have used in sessions and have suggested the children implement in other environments are as follows:

- Having an awareness of the children's individual sensory sensitivities
- Taking breaks when the children's attention is waning
- Making sure that there are activities that include motion and gross motor work in each lesson
- Using movement as refocusing and transition activities
- Working with an occupational therapist who is trained in sensory integration

Building our own awareness of the sensory system as it impacts on language, process, and social ability has helped us facilitate children more successfully. We recommend that all adults looking to support a child's social development keep sensory awareness as a daily part of their planning. When you see that you are losing a group or an individual child, it is better to give a sensory solution at that time than to push through the activity or attempt to stop the behavior. As a teacher, sometimes you find yourself saying, "Come on, let's just get this done." Instead, give everyone a break to refocus and return to the activity. The following is a list of cues that children's sensory systems are becoming overwhelmed and some quick things to suggest that will help them focus and finish the activities or lesson.

Stuff Kids Do to Regulate Themselves

- Tap pens
- Rock in chair
- Squirm on seat
- Talk
- Stare
- Chew on pencil, fingers, gum
- Take longer to answer question
- Tap feet
- Turn around
- Increase in negative affect
- Bug and pick on others
- Disorientated response

Things to Suggest

These suggestions are things that are good to put in at times of transition, breaks in the middle of activities, or during times when children are waiting and their attention starts to wane. Make sure that they are short so you do not lose the children. If the refocusing exercises are too long, the children will lose track of the fact that they are refocusing. A few seconds to a minute is all that is needed to regulate and redirect them back to the activity at hand.

- Stretch
- Pull up on your chair
- Push down on your desk
- Squeeze your head
- Chew on straw or water bottle
- Squeeze your hands
- Push on wall
- Carry something heavy

How to Use This Book

The following is an outline of the sections in each unit, describing what they contain and how to best implement the activities.

UNIT

- The units are in sequential order.
- You should start at the beginning of the book and work your way through to the end; the units are designed to be completed in order.
- You may choose to skip some of the beginning concepts if you feel your children are past them. However, we suggest the beginning chapters still be introduced to the children so they can learn some of the Wanna Play terms that are used throughout the curriculum.

SOCIAL GOALS

- The goals are listed in each section of the book. This is done so that it is clear what goals each section targets. The Social Interactive Checklist can be used to assess the child's present skill level and to pick the goal appropriate for the child.
- Use these social goals as a guide when developing a child's program and writing educational plans.

LESSON

- Each lesson builds on the previous lesson.
- Each lesson can also be extracted individually as needed.
- Some children will have some of the skills already, but they are worth reviewing.

Introduction/Overview

- Purpose
- Introduction of the concept for the adult

- Our opinion on it
- The importance of the skills
- Background information
- Introduction of terms

Teaching Concepts

- The main idea of the lesson
- The skills to be taught
- Belief system the lesson is based on
- The benefit of learning the lesson

Attitudinal Approach

- Things the adult should remember when going over the lesson
- Attitudinal perceptions of the teacher
- Attitudes the adults should adopt
- The attitude that should be projected to the student so he or she can take his or her cue from the adult

Lesson Objectives

- Each objective is written in measurable outcomes, and frequency and duration can be determined based on the needs of the group.
- Observable behaviors
- Outcomes of the lesson
- Changes in the child
- Skills or concepts the child will learn and use

Lesson Introduction

- This section will help the children organize the concepts by giving visual supports that help them retain the concepts.
- Use leading questions to help children develop lists and concept maps. Examples can found within each lesson introduction.

Concept Mapping

- Draw bubble maps on a board so the children can have a visual understanding of the layout.
- Example:
  - What do we do with our friends? Play
  - How do we play? Friendly
  - What do you use to play friendly? Use sweet words, use listening, use safe body, use safe toys
- Use pictures to help the children come up with the specific word on the bubble maps.

- If a child gives an answer that is not on the map, use a leading question to redirect the child back to the topic being discussed. Do not tell the child that any answer is wrong unless it is a negative concept.
- Feel free to add related answers children think of to the bubble map, even if they are not listed in the curriculum. Try to make sure the words and concepts added support the concept map as it is being developed.

Brainstorming and List Making

We use this technique to access what a child already knows about a concept and use it as a springboard to develop new ideas. As with concept mapping, we are helping the children to tap into their memory and to add new information to what they already know.

- Introduce the concept with a clear heading (example: "Deciding Who Goes First").
- Use pictures as visual support if needed.
- Have children list as many things as they can on the concept.
- Redirect children when they go off topic by using positive leading questions.
- Use questions as an assessment tool to find out children's concept development of the importance of friendship (example: "Whom do we look at?").
- Encourage children to think of all the people that they may talk to or interact with during the day. Be sure to include peers and adults in all environments—home, educational, social, and so forth.
- Help children to think about the times that they need to listen to others for directions or information, look at others when they want something, or want others to listen to them. Use different situations as examples.

Word Defining

- Word-defining lesson introductions use similar procedures and strategies to brainstorming and list making.
- Have children share as many definitions as they can think of and list them all.
- When the list is finished, create a definition as a group, similar to the example given in the curriculum.

Activities

- The activities provided in this book are geared toward abilities in children ages 4 to 10. Some activities, such as coloring in sweet words, are more appropriate for younger children; activities such as friendship cards are geared toward older children with more expressive abilities such as writing. Consider the ages of the children and their abilities when choosing the activities for your group.
- In the activities section of each lesson, there are games and projects for all types of learners. We suggest that the teacher choose a balance of gross motor, art, game, role-play, writing, group, and individual activities to target all learners in the class.
- There are built-in repetitions of skill learning to utilize repetition as an effective learning tool.

- Use at least three or four activities from each lesson to help children internalize each skill.
- All of the activities listed are also good to use separately as fun skill builders throughout the children's day.
- Each activity will outline the following:
  - Purpose
  - Materials
  - Preparation
  - Procedure

Friendship Cards

Purpose

The friendship cards are used as a visual reminder for the children to reinforce the concept that has been taught. Many children can internalize the information they learn in a social lesson and even demonstrate the ability to use a skill when discussing an activity or in a synthetic role-playing situation. The difficulty lies in using that skill or strategy in real-time social interaction. The friendship cards are a toolbox of choices that children can draw from and use in the heat of the moment.

Materials

Friendship cards are located in Appendix A. Each card is titled, and there is a master list to help keep track of the cards used in each lesson. We suggest using loose-leaf rings or key chains to hold the cards together. We also suggest the cards be glued to index cards for stability.

Preparation: Copy and cut a set of cards for each child. Glue the cards to index cards and hole-punch them. Choose a location to store the cards that is accessible to the entire class.

Procedure

1. Introduce the cards as a tool. Give a brief description of what the cards are and how they will be used. Show the children where the cards will be located so that they can find them later. Have children decorate their cover card and put it on their ring. This can be done as part of the first friendship cards lesson.

2. Give each child the card corresponding to the lesson. Have children review the information learned in the lesson and use the visual aids created in the lesson introduction to fill out their card. Most cards correspond directly with the specific lesson introduction.

3. Have children write or draw to fill in the card. Encourage children to illustrate the card with examples that will help them to remember and recall the information on the card.

4. Have children store cards in an accessible location.

Using Cards in Social Situations

1. When a social situation arises where a child is having difficulty remembering the social lessons learned, redirect the child to get her or his card.

2. Encourage the child to find the card that has the strategy that would help him or her in that specific situation. This step also gives the child a chance to calm down and move away from the scene if he or she is overwhelmed and having difficulty staying calm.

3. Help the child find the strategy that would help her or him in that situation, and then encourage the child to go back to her or his friend and use the chosen tool or social phrase.

Generalization and Consistency

Not all lessons have or need strategies. For those that do, the strategy should be followed to the letter. Some strategies can be used for multiple lessons.

- Key phrases
- Transitions

In this section of the unit, you will find suggested strategies and techniques that should be integrated into the classroom curriculum and even in the school culture. This strategies are geared toward incidental teaching. They are based on the concept that the moment children begin to struggle with a social situation is the moment they should be reminded of the social strategies and techniques they have been taught.

Social Interaction Checklist

The following Social Interaction Checklist is designed to help identify the social strengths and weaknesses of each child. Have parents and other people in each child's life answer the questions and use the results to choose the goals for each child. Some children will have different social goals for different social environments based on social and sensory experiences. These goals have been laid out in a progression, and we suggest working to them in order from Eye Contact and Interaction to Social Awareness.

Name: _____

Start Date: _____

Social Goal	Emerging	Present	Mastered	Not Applicable
Interaction				
Child will make eye contact with peers and adults when they are requesting interaction from the child.				
Child will use eye contact as a cue when they are attempting to engage others in interaction.				
Child will maintain conversational eye contact for the entire verbal conversation with peer or adult.				
Child will maintain eye contact and hold interest with a speaker in a group discussion or classroom setting for the length of the presentation.				
Child will retain information from a speaker in a group discussion or classroom setting for the length of the presentation.				
Child will use the skills taught to maintain focus and attention in a group environment interaction.				
Child will choose activities that include others over solitary activities.				
Child will engage in reciprocal activities with another child.				

Social Goal	Emerging	Present	Mastered	Not Applicable
Child will engage in reciprocal activities with an adult.				
Child will join activities with others when invited.				
Child will choose (prompted/facilitated) to complete a game with another child.				
Child will choose (unprompted/unfacilitated) to complete a game with another child.				
Child will choose (prompted/facilitated) to complete a game with a group.				
Child will choose (unprompted/unfacilitated) to complete a game with a group.				
Child will choose (prompted/facilitated) to complete a multistep task.				
Child will choose (unprompted/unfacilitated) to complete a multistep task.				
Child will sustain eye contact throughout the length of an interaction with peers and adults.				
Child will engage in interactive turn-taking with peers and facilitators.				
Communication				
Child will use a system to clearly communicate their wants, needs and ideas to others.				
Child will initiate and respond to greetings and salutations from peers and adults without prompting.				
Child will use eye contact and a requesting phrase simultaneously to request for a toy or game.				
Child will communicate with peers and adults original topics and ideas instead of perseverating on one topic or idea.				
Child will use sweet words and phrases when requesting from peers and adults.				
Child will use a kind, polite tone of voice when communicating with others.				
Child will build an awareness of when to tell lengthy stories and when to be concise.				
Child will inquire about other's interests and talk to them.				
Child will maintain a conversation with a peer or an adult by using verbal cues, such as comments, questions, verbal turn-taking, and transitional phrases.				

(Continued)

(Continued)

Social Goal	Emerging	Present	Mastered	Not Applicable
Child will restate him or herself when they are understood and ask others to repeat themselves when they do not understand.				
Child will stay on topic when contributing to a group discussion in a classroom setting.				
Child will use a natural fluctuation of tone and pitch when communicating.				
Child will understand nonverbal cues of others that indicate whether someone is interested in the conversation.				
Child will choose the topics of conversation that are appropriate for the setting that he or she is in.				
Child will express past experiences and future ideas with description and detail.				
Child will use appropriate conversation space when talking to others.				
Child will use questions to continue a conversation and to inquire about the other person.				
Child will wait his or her turn to speak in a conversation.				
Child will end a conversation appropriately.				
Child will use an appropriate conversation starter.				
Child will use prompted phrases to initiate with others in a group setting.				
Child will use prompted phrases to initiate conversation with a peer.				
Child will use prompts to make suggestions to peers during group activities.				
Child will make positive suggestions to peers of original ideas during group activities.				
Child will use verbal cues such as comments, questions and transitional phrases to continue a conversation to introduce own ideas into a conversation.				
Child will use positive proactive phrases to let his or her wants or needs known, instead of shouting "no" or "stop" or engaging in another negative behavior.				
Child will use positive language when engaging peers and adults in a verbal interaction.				

Social Goal	Emerging	Present	Mastered	Not Applicable
Appropriate Behavior and Flexibility				
Child will choose a positive, proactive affect in all social situations.				
Child will use sweet words and a kind voice in social situations with peers and adults.				
Child will use language and a calm affect in a conflict situation.				
Child will use resolutions such as making trades, deals, sharing, and brainstorming new choices.				
Child will use visual, verbal, and physical techniques to calm him or herself in a conflict situation.				
Child will use positive interactions and behaviors to get attention.				
Child will use sensory input to gain and maintain control of emotional level.				
Child will respect personal space of peers and adults during group activity.				
Child will use strategies taught to increase his ability to use socially appropriate conversation skills including kind words, kind voice, socially appropriate topics and increased flexibility to engage in a conversation with transitions to other topics.				
Child will use strategies taught to increase his ability to use socially appropriate conversation skills including kind words, kind voice, socially appropriate topics and increased flexibility to engage in a conversation with transitions to other topics.				
Child will use strategies to maintain a calm affect when challenged, to ensure that taught strategies can be utilized to increase the child's ability to resolve challenging situations.				
Child will express anger and frustration via socially appropriate means, such as appropriate language.				
Use taught strategies to resolve conflicts before approaching an adult or seeking facilitation.				
Child will be able to adapt to changes in the environment, using taught strategies to maintain a calm affect.				

(Continued)

(Continued)

Social Goal	Emerging	Present	Mastered	Not Applicable
Child will adapt to changing play themes using strategies taught to increase flexibility during play interactions, instead of leaving the interaction or becoming frustrated.				
Child will listen to prompts and strategies mid-interaction from a facilitator in order to increase positive responses from peers be more successful in a situation.				
Child will recognize emotions and express emotions via a socially appropriate means.				
Recognize and interpret emotions of others and respond in a socially appropriate way.				
Play				
Child will allow expansion of repetitious play by a peer or an adult.				
Child will use toys as a way of interacting with others instead of isolating himself/herself from others during play.				
Child will play alone, with no awareness of or involvement with other children. (Solitary play)[a]				
Child will watch others play without entering the activities. (Onlooker Play)[a]				
Child will play with similar objects clearly beside other children with slight acknowledgement of the others. (Parallel play)[a]				
Child will engage in unstructured interactive play with similar toys with other children. (Associative play)[a]				
Child will engage in structured group play with rules and goals. (Cooperative play)[a]				
Child will invite a peer to play with them.				
Child will join another child or group of children if asked in play, game or activity.				
Child will ask to join another child or group of children in play, game or activity.				
Child will attempt to join another child or group of children in play by making a suggestion to add on to the game or activity.				
Child will follow a play theme until game or activity is finished.				
Child will use show good sportsmanship in a game by cheering on a peer.				

Social Goal	Emerging	Present	Mastered	Not Applicable
Child will learn to trade, take turns, share, or pick a new toy with facilitation.				
Child will learn to trade, take turns, share, or pick a new toy unfacilitated.				
Child will use taught strategies to expand a play theme and to include new ideas in a group play setting.				
Social Awareness				
Child will identify his or her own strengths and needs and that of their peers.				
Child will use encouraging phrases and actions in games and activities with peers.				
Child will verbally show appreciation for others by using "please," "thank you," and apologies.				
Child will physically show appreciation of others by including others and sharing.				
Child will respect and support their friends without using bossy or motherly tones.				
Child will positively express to others their ability to complete a task when being over-facilitated or babied by an adult or peer.				
Child will identify situations that are fair and the same and fair and not the same.				
Child will be able to list the outcomes of being kind to others or being mean to others.				
Child will use skills, organizing others, giving directions, listening to ideas, and encouraging participation to lead a group.				
Child will learn about the various roles in a group and the skills necessary to successfully work in each role.				
Child will explain his or her attitude or perception of a person or situation verbally instead of just using negative facial expression and body posturing.				
Child will develop the ability to consider all possibilities of someone's intention instead of jumping to one conclusion.				
A child will ask a peer or adult to explain the emotions and motivations behind their behavior if a child cannot figure it out on their own.				
Child will stay on topic when contributing to a group discussion in a classroom setting.				

(Continued)

(Continued)

Social Goal	Emerging	Present	Mastered	Not Applicable
Child will respect personal space of peers and adults during a group activity.				
Child will use the skills taught to maintain focus and attention in a group environment.				
Child will learn to ask for help when needed when he or she is not able to listen or attend.				
Child will increase his or her ability to participate in a group by learning how to listen in a group.				
Child will use visual supports to increase participation and contributions to a group project.				
Child will learn how to listen to others ideas and show respect for their idea even though they may not agree.				
Child will read social cues to engage in conversation or activity with peers by understanding what the social cues mean.				
Body Space Awareness				
Child will respect personal space of peers and adults.				
Child will use sensory suggestions when prompted by an adult.				
Child will use sensory suggestions when needed without prompting.				
Child will understand concepts from the Alert program and use sensory suggestions to change engine level.				
Child will ask before they touch, hug, or hold the hand of a peer or adult.				
Child will begin a social interaction by using an appropriate greeting instead of hugging or using another physical gesture.				
Child will use appropriate levels of movement and energy for different activities and environments.				
Child will use prompted sensory suggestions as a break then continue in the interaction or activity.				

a. Parten, M. B. (1932). Social participation among preschool children. *Journal of Abnormal Psychology, 27,* 243–269.

UNIT 1

Discovering Social Skills

The skills needed to make positive friendships should be taught to all children and are skills that will help them interact in relationships throughout their lives. Often, defining and discussing who friends are and the importance of friendship will help increase children's appreciation of their friends. The children will then make attempts to strive for better friendships with the friends they already have. Teaching the skills in this unit will build a basis of understanding for children of why we want to learn the skills in the following units. Building better relationships and having friends is the reason we want to learn to use kind words, look at our friends, and listen to our friends; learn how to play games; and learn to work in a group.

SOCIAL GOALS

- Child will initiate and respond to greetings and salutations from peers and adults without prompting.
- Child will restate himself or herself when not understood and will ask others to repeat themselves when he or she does not understand.
- Child will physically show appreciation of others by including others and sharing.
- Child will invite a peer to play with her or him.
- Child will use a system to clearly communicate his or her wants, needs, and ideas to others.

Lesson 1.1

What Are Social Skills?

Introduction/Overview

The introduction of this unit begins with defining both *friend* and *friendship*. This allows children to think more specifically about what a friend means and what they need to do to build friendships with others. Begin using the term *friend* whenever you are referring to others in the group. Children may not necessarily consider each child a friend, but they will benefit from using positive friendship skills whenever they interact with others.

Teaching Concepts

- We need to include others in what we do in order to build friendships.
- Things are more fun to do when we are with our friends.
- A friendship can begin with the first hello.

Attitudinal Approach

- Observing the children and complimenting their attempts at using positive friendship skills is the best way to reinforce the concepts we want them to learn.
- Even the children who prefer to be by themselves will benefit from learning these concepts for when they have to interact with others.
- Support the children with positive verbal reinforcement if they need to be encouraged to include others and think of them as friends.

Lesson Objectives

- Children will list what they need to say and do to make friends with others.
- Children will participate in making a list of ways to include others in their games and activities.
- Children will learn phrases and actions that make being a friend fun.

Lesson Introduction

Brainstorm for Key Concepts

Have children develop lists to refer to by asking specific questions. Use the directions found on page 11 in the "How to Use This Book" section. *Time:* 10–15 minutes.

- What is friendship?
- Who are your friends?
- What are fun things to do with friends?
- Why are friends great?

For nonreaders: Use stick figures to represent the friends on the children's lists with names written above. For the list of things we do with friends, use the pictures of toys from the "Picture Flashcards" (page 179) in Appendix B.

Activities

 ### 1.1A Friendship Collage

Time: 15–20 minutes

Purpose: This activity will expand on the ideas children think of to do with their friends. Children will often choose only one or two things to play. Using pictures can help them think of fun new things to play.

Materials: Old toy catalogs and children's magazines, scissors, glue sticks, large piece of 8½ × 11 pieces of white paper, letters cut out of construction paper to spell *friendship*

Preparation: Gather supplies.

Procedure:

1. Explain that the children are to look through the catalogs or magazines for pictures of toys, games, or children playing together.

2. Have them cut out the pictures they find. Help with the cutting if necessary.

3. The pictures can then be glued on individual sheets or on one large sheet of paper if children are working as a group.

4. You can have them glue the pictures onto the *friendship* letters first, and then glue the letters on the poster.

5. Write a heading on the poster. Example: "Things We Do With Friends."

 ### 1.1B Friendship Acrostic Poem

Time: 15–20 minutes

Purpose: Brainstorming friendship words will begin to help the children think of all the ways to be a good friend. This activity can either be done as a group or individually.

Materials: Large paper for poster, construction paper, or white 8½ × 11 paper

Preparation: Cut the letters to the word *friendship* out of construction paper and hang them vertically down a poster-size piece of paper, or write the word *friendship* vertically down an 8½ × 11 piece of paper for each child.

Procedure:

1. Have children brainstorm as a group or individually think of friendship words that begin with each letter of the word *friendship*. Often, using books about friendship can also help them be more creative in the words they may choose.

2. Use the lists that were made in the lesson introduction as reminders of friend-ship words.

3. Write the words next to the letter, using it as the first letter in the word.

4. Hang the poster or individual poems in the room as reminders of friendship.

1.1C Friends 2-by-2 Game

Time: 10–15 minutes

Purpose: This is a great game for the children to begin interacting with other children, find out something about a friend, and become more comfortable with pretending.

Materials: Equal number of cards with 2 of each animal written on individual cards.

Example: 2 lions, 2 bears, 2 dogs, etc.

Preparation: Make the animal cards. If reading is still challenging, write the words and have a picture of the animal.

Procedure:

1. Have each child pick a card.

2. Make sure all the cards are used so each child is matched with another child.

3. Explain that they must act out the animal on their card and find a friend who is being the same animal they are. They cannot ask their friends; they have to figure it out by what the other children are doing.

4. Once they find their "twin" animal, they can talk. They must find out one thing about the other child. You may need to help by giving them a category or question.

Example: "What is your favorite TV show?"

"What is your favorite game?"

5. When they have finished finding out the answer to the questions, have the children share what they found out about their friend with the group.

1.1D Friendship Cards— Discovering Social Skills

Time: 15 minutes

Purpose: The friendship cards are used as a visual reminder for the children to reinforce the concept that has been taught.

Materials: Friendship Cards in Appendix A:

- Friendship
- Why Friends Are Great

Preparation: See directions in "How to Use This Book" on page 12.

Procedure: See directions in "How to Use This Book" on page 12.

Generalization and Consistency

- Use the term *friend* whenever you are referring to the children interacting with their peers. This will encourage the thoughts that we want to make friendships and that friends are fun.
- Verbally acknowledge all positive interactions and point out all use of friendship skills when children are interacting.
- Make all activities opportunities to build friendships.

Lesson 1.2

Making New Friends

Introduction/Overview

The way we interact with new friends can be very different from how we interact with friends we have known for a while. This lesson will help the children initiate interactions and friendships and learn how to differentiate these relationships from friendships that they have already made with others.

Teaching Concepts

- Using greetings initiates interactions with others.
- We need to say certain things to make friends.
- We need to do certain things to make friends.

Attitudinal Approach

- Friendship skills need to be taught and modeled.
- Just because the children may not know the things to do or say to be a friend does not mean they do not want to make friends.
- Even though some children may play alone, they will benefit from learning how to make friends.

Lesson Objectives

- Children will learn different ways to make friends.
- Children will learn different places to look for friends and ways to tell if others want to be their friend.
- Learning things about others is a way to make friends.

Lesson Introduction

Brainstorm for Key Concepts

Have children develop lists to refer to by asking specific questions. Use the directions found on page 11 in the "How to Use This Book" section. *Time:* 10–15 minutes.

- What are ways to say hello?
- What are ways to say good-bye?
- What are the words to say to introduce yourself?

Activities

1.2A Meatball

Time: 5–15 minutes

Purpose: Children will spend time asking questions about the people in their group. It will help them find out more about the other children.

Materials: Small ball, polyspots or sit-upons (if needed)

Preparation: Set up spots in a circle for children to sit on.

Procedure:

1. With all children sitting in a circle, have them take turns passing the ball to one another.

2. Have children then say the name of the person they are passing to and ask that person a question about herself or himself.

3. Give suggestions of what to ask if the children are having trouble thinking of what to say. Examples: Name, favorite food, person who threw the ball, that person's favorite food, or the person they are going to throw the ball to next.

1.2B Friend, Friend, What Do You See?

Time: 15–30 minutes

This activity can be broken up into two to three parts if the attention span of the group is an issue.

Purpose: This activity is based on the book *Brown Bear, Brown Bear, What Do You See?* by Eric Carl. Do the activity as explained and then adapt the activity to allow the children to look at their friends and notice things about them.

Materials: The book *Brown Bear, Brown Bear, What Do You See?* by Bill Martin, Jr., and Eric Carle, Worksheet 1.1 "Puppets for Brown Bear" (page 166) in Appendix B, sticks for the puppets, crayon or markers, scissors, and tape

Preparation: Make copies of the puppets, enough for each child to color at least one.

Procedure:

1. Read the "Brown Bear" book.

2. Have each child color and cut out at least one puppet. Make sure you have at least one of every animal in the story.

3. Tape the puppets to a stick.

4. Reread the story. Every time a new animal is mentioned, have the children raise their puppet. The children are usually very familiar with the story and enjoy saying the story while you read.

5. Then have the children take turns saying, "Friend, friend, what do you see?" looking at one of the children in the group.

6. The child they are looking at must then say one thing he or she sees when he or she looks at the other child.

Example: "I see a happy smile looking at me."

"I see blonde hair looking at me."

7. If the children have started to learn things about each other, encourage them to say the things they know about the other child.

Example: "I see a kid who loves cars looking at me."

1.2C Introduce Yourself

Time: 10–15 minutes

Purpose: Using the words we know to say hello and let people know we want to be friends. Learn that we say hello differently to different people in different places.

Materials: "People Flashcards" and "Place Flashcards" found in Appendix B

Preparation: Cut out cards in the appendix. Draw pictures on cards or help the children to read the cards for their turn.

Procedure:

1. Have each child take a turn and pick a card from the people pile and the place pile.

2. Role-play saying hello, pretending another child is that person.

3. Discuss the different places and appropriate interactions for each place.

1.2D Making Friends Worksheet

Time: 10–15 minutes

Purpose: This activity is suited for use in a group or one-to-one session. The statements or questions listed will help the child begin to think of who he or she might want to attempt being friends with and what to say when he or she decides to try to make a friend.

Materials: Worksheets 1.2 (Making Friends) on page 171 and 1.3 (You and Your Friend) on page 172 in Appendix B

Preparation: Make copies of both worksheets for each child.

Procedure:

1. Give each child a set of worksheets.
2. Explain the questions or statements. Give suggestions for possible responses.
3. Also explain that the person they are thinking of may be someone they have talked to before or someone who they just think it might be fun to be friends with.
4. Have them draw a picture of themselves and that person on the last page doing something fun together.

1.2E Lifestories Game by FNDI Limited Partnership

Time: See game rules.

Purpose: This is a great game to find out more about other people. Different questions encourage players to share stories and facts about themselves and their families. Basic reading is helpful. If there are some stronger readers in the group, encourage the children to ask each other for help reading if they need it.

Materials: Game

Preparation: Read the directions to be able to explain to the children. Sometimes this is a great opportunity to let the children learn how to play on their own as a group activity.

Procedure: Follow the directions included in the game.

1.2F Friendship Cards— Discovering Social Skills

Time: 10–15 minutes

Purpose: The friendship cards are used as a visual reminder for the children to reinforce the concept that has been taught.

Materials: Friendship Cards in Appendix A:

- Ways to Say Hello
- Ways to Introduce Yourself

Preparation: See directions in "How to Use This Book" on page 12.

Procedure: See directions in "How to Use This Book" on page 12.

Generalization and Consistency

- Acknowledge any attempts of the children to interact with someone new.
- Provide opportunities for the children to get another child's attention by calling his or her name. This will help the children to learn the names of the other children.
- Remember interesting facts about the children and use them during conversations so they will see how great it is to know things about people to make friends.

Lesson 1.3

Building Friendships

Introduction/Overview

Teaching the skills to build friendships is as important as teaching how to make friendships. It takes effort to keep friendships going and to try to make deeper relationships with others. This lesson expands on the skills learned in the first lesson to build friendships with peers.

Teaching Concepts

- Making friends is fun.
- Making friends takes effort.
- Thinking about our friends helps to make friendships.
- Finding out about our friends is part of making friends.

Attitudinal Approach

- Making the extra effort to be a friend needs our positive guidance and support.
- Friendship skills need to be taught step by step.
- Help children to learn the importance of friends by talking about the friendships in our lives.
- Acknowledge children when they are using positive friendship skills with others.

Lesson Objectives

- Children will learn the step-by-step skills needed to make friendships.
- Children will learn the benefit of making the extra effort to build friendships.
- Children will learn questions to ask to build friendships.

Lesson Introduction

Concept Map—What Do We Need to Do to Build Friendships?

Have the children help develop a concept map (see Figure 1.1) by asking leading questions. Use the directions found on page 11 in the "How to Use This Book" section. *Time:* 10–15 minutes.

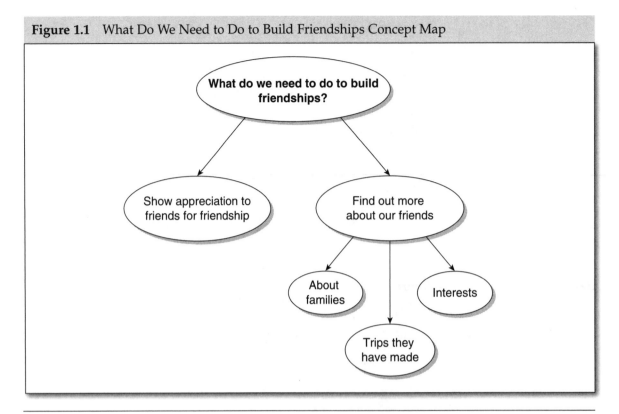

Figure 1.1 What Do We Need to Do to Build Friendships Concept Map

Activities

1.3A Friend Bingo

Time: 10–15 minutes

Purpose: This activity helps children learn questions to ask to make friends and find out more things about our friends.

Materials: Worksheet 1.6 Friend Bingo on page 175 in Appendix B, markers or crayons

Preparation: Add pictures to the bingo sheet to help the children who are not reading yet.

Procedure:

1. Give each child a worksheet and a marker or crayon.

2. Have the all the children walk around and ask the other children who has things on the sheet or who has done the things on the sheet.

3. They can either ask until they have four in a row or fill the whole sheet.

1.3B Gift of Friendship

Time: 10–15 minutes

Purpose: To have children think of special things they can do or say to friends to show their appreciation for their friendship. This activity can focus on building friendships within the group and also help the children to think of other friendships in their lives.

Materials: Worksheet 1.7 Gift of Friendship on page 176 in Appendix B, marker or crayons

Preparation: Make copies of the worksheet.

Procedure:

1. Discuss or make a list of different things to say or things to do to say thank you to a friend for being a friend.

2. Encourage children to use words of appreciation as gifts instead of toys.

3. Have the children think of a friend they want to give a gift to and decorate the gift with the words and any additional decoration they want to add.

4. You can use this activity again at holidays or for birthday celebrations.

1.3C Charades for Kids by Pressman

Time: See game rules.

Purpose: This is a great game to help young children build confidence about interacting with friends so they can have the confidence to approach others to make friendships grow.

Materials: Charades for Kids board game

Preparation: None

Procedure: Play the game using the instructions included with the game.

1.3D Write a Letter to a Friend

Time: 5–10 minutes

Purpose: This activity is a great reflection of what children appreciate about the friends they have just made. It can be used after the children have been together for a short while or a whole school year.

Materials: Copies of the Worksheet 1.8 Letter to a Friend on page 177 in Appendix B

Preparation: Make copies of the worksheet.

Procedure:

1. Explain the purpose of the letter and that this is a time to thank the friend or friends for the opportunity of meeting them and becoming friends.

2. If working with a group of children, encourage them to choose someone from that group.

3. Collect all the letters at the end and hand them out later or put them in backpacks to take home.

4. Explain that we want to keep who we wrote to or how many letters we got to ourselves.

5. This helps to minimize the possibility of hurting the feelings of children who did not receive as many letters.

6. Note who did not receive any letters and use this as an opportunity to teach more friendship skills.

1.3E Friendship Cards— Discovering Social Skills

Time: 10–15 minutes

Purpose: The friendship cards are used as a visual reminder for the children to reinforce the concept that has been taught.

Materials: Friendship Cards in Appendix A:

- Ways to Show Appreciation
- Things We Can Find Out About Friends

Preparation: See directions in "How to Use This Book" on page 12.

Procedure: See directions in "How to Use This Book" on page 12.

Generalization and Consistency

- Finding out information about the people we want to be friends with is a great way to make friends. Prompt the children with questions to ask others to find out more about them.
- Working in pairs encourages friendships and helps children find out more about the other children.
- Use the common interests of the children as ways of linking them to each other. Example: Group by "dinosaur lovers" for an activity.

 esson 1.4

Relationships With Different Types of Friends

Introduction/Overview

Children have the opportunity to meet friends in different places and to make friendships with different types of friends. Some people are easier to be friends with than others, and we also have different types of relationships with different friends. Also, having different types of friends and different types of relationships requires us to think about what things we want to do or say with which friends.

Teaching Concepts

- There are different types of people in the world, and relationships may be different too.
- We want to look for certain qualities in friends.
- We want to have certain qualities to be a good friend.
- Treating others with kindness is the best way to be a friend.

Attitudinal Approach

- Some of the children may not understand that they need to think about appropriate interactions depending on who they are interacting with and where they are.
- Everyone has positive qualities.
- Everyone can learn to be more positive when making friends.

Lesson Objectives

- Children will learn the different types of friends.
- Children will discover positive qualities in themselves.
- Children will learn what positive qualities to look for in others to build friendships.

Lesson Introduction

Concept Map—Types of Friends

Have the children help develop a concept map (see Figure 1.2) by asking leading questions. Use the directions found on page 11 in the "How to Use This Book" section. *Time:* 10–15 minutes.

Figure 1.2 Types of Friends Concept Map

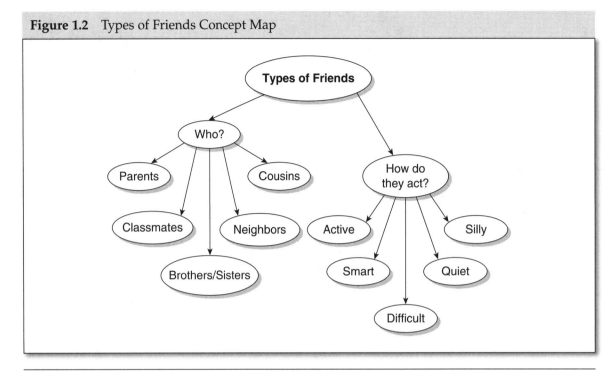

Activities

1.4A School Friends and Best Friends Cartoons

Time: 15–20 minutes

Purpose: To help children think of new and different things to say and do with friends. This will also help them differentiate how well we know people and what it means to be a best friend.

Materials: Worksheets 1.4 (Best Friends) on page 173 and 1.5 (School Friends) on page 174 in Appendix B, markers, crayons

Preparation: Make copies of the worksheet.

Procedure:

1. Either brainstorm lists or talk about the things we do with our friends at school and the things we do with our best friends.

2. Refer back to the concept map in the lesson introduction to talk about different types of friends and how they act.

3. Have each child think of something she or he would do with each type of friend and what she or he would be saying.

4. Have the children color a cartoon for each.

5. Older children may want several cartoon boxes to make a comic strip.

1.4B Friendship Quilt

Time: 15–20 minutes

Purpose: This activity will introduce the concept of positive qualities. You may need to define positive qualities to the children. You can also substitute "good things we like about others" or "great ways to be a friend" to help children think about the wonderful positive friendship qualities they have and their friends have.

Materials: Worksheet 1.9 Friendship Quilt on page 178 in Appendix B, markers, large paper

Preparation: Make copies of the quilt squares.

Procedure:

1. Brainstorm the great things about the children and their friends. You can ask why they like to be friends. Also point out what makes them good friends.

2. Have the children choose a quality, write it on the square, then have them draw a picture of themselves and their friend doing what they have picked.

3. Write "Friendship Quilt" on a large paper and hang it on the wall.

4. When the children finish their quilt square, have them glue it to the quilt.

5. Have the children make several squares to fill the quilt.

1.4C Group It

Time: 10–15 minutes

Purpose: This activity encourages interaction between the children in the group and helps teach the idea that the more we learn about our friends, the more fun we will have with them.

Materials: Index cards with a different category written on each card. Choose a variety of categories so that the children will be able to easily think of an idea.

Preparation: Make the cards. If reading is still challenging, use pictures along with the words.

Procedure:

1. Have a child pick a card and read or tell what the card says.

2. Explain that the children must then walk around and find the other children who like the same thing from that category.

3. If food is the category, then explain that they must all think of their favorite food and find others who like the same thing.

1.4D Friendship Cards—Discovering Social Skills

Time: 10–15 minutes

Purpose: The friendship cards are used as a visual reminder for the children to reinforce the concept that has been taught.

Materials: Friendship Cards in Appendix A:

- Our Friends
- How Our Friends Act

Preparation: See directions in "How to Use This Book" on page 12.

Procedure: See directions in "How to Use This Book" on page 12.

Generalization and Consistency

- Acknowledge any and all attempts children make to show appreciation to a friend.
- When a child does something for another child or for you, show your appreciation for their effort by saying, "Thank you; you are such a good friend to do (whatever he or she did) or say (whatever he or she said)."
- Encourage children to ask questions when interacting with another child. Prompt the idea or the exact words if necessary.
- When children begin to make a friendship, acknowledge it by telling them what they have done to try to be a friend.

Using Appropriate Eye Contact for Interaction

"The eyes are the windows to the soul," the proverb says. That is why eye contact deserves a unit of its own. This is the beginning of all interactions. Eye contact with infants is the key form of communication. It is how they learn about the world around them. Children use eye contact to develop their perception of trust and what is a constant in the world. Through the years of development, children use eye contact to explore and learn. It is key in learning the forms of communication such as language, gesture, and expression. Without eye contact, our ability to gain information about the world around us would be limited, and the possibility of social mistakes would be greatly increased.

The key to success in this program is an emphasis on developing eye-contact frequency and duration. There are many factors that come into play when we see children who are not making eye contact. Some of these include visual sensitivity, auditory sensitivity, sensory overstimulation, or even a lack of understanding of the role of eye contact in interaction. We need to remember, as those responsible for the social development of a child, that if the child is not making eye contact, he or she is not engaging, attending, or focusing.

Children are tricky when it comes to avoiding eye contact. They are more vested in avoidance than we are. This avoidance is a safety mechanism for them in some form, and therefore, they will try to hold onto it as much as they can.

SOCIAL GOALS

- The child will understand the importance of eye contact as an interactive tool.
- The child will make eye contact when listening to adults and peers.

- The child will make eye contact when making a request to an adult or child.
- The child will make eye contact when telling stories and relaying experiences to adults and other children.

Lesson 2.1

What Is Eye Contact?

Introduction/Overview

In this lesson, we explore the meaning and importance of eye contact. We want teachers to use this time to assess children's understanding of what it means to make eye contact or look at others.

Teaching Concepts

- Eye contact is looking into someone's eyes in a way that has meaning.
- Eye contact is helpful and important.
- Eye contact is an important component of communication and is needed to increase attention and focus.
- Eye contact needs to be practiced in controlled situations to make it easier in natural environments.
- Sometimes we need to work on making eye contact to get better at it.
- Eye contact is held as much as possible for the whole of the interaction.

Attitudinal Approach

- Although eye contact is challenging and children will resist it, we still need to teach it with a positive attitude.
- This concept needs to be worked on until the children are able to use eye contact effectively.
- We cannot assume children will have a conscious awareness of what eye contact is.
- Making and holding eye contact is not always easy and is often taken for granted.
- Not making eye contact is not always a sign of insolence, guilt, or ignoring.

Lesson Objectives

- Children will identify looking into another's eyes as eye contact.
- Children will identify whom to look at when interacting.
- Children will have experience with making eye contact for a long duration.

Lesson Introduction

Brainstorm for Key Concepts

Have children develop lists to refer to by asking specific questions. Use the directions found on page 11 in the "How to Use This Book" section. *Time:* 10–15 minutes.

- Whom do we look at?
- Why do we look at other people?
- Why do other people look at us?

Activities

2.1A Staring Contest

Time: 5–10 minutes

Purpose: This activity enables the children to have the physical experience of making and holding eye contact.

Materials: None

Preparation: None

Procedure:

1. Have children pair off.

2. Explain to the children that they need to look into their friend's eyes until you say stop.

3. Children are allowed to blink, but not to talk (they will ask).

4. Start with 15 seconds and go up as time goes on.

5. Make it fun!

2.1B Silly Glasses

Time: 10–15 minutes

Purpose: Many children need a little visual interest to help them to attend. Visual distracters in their environment make it difficult for them to cue in and stay with someone. This activity is a fun, silly way to help.

Materials: Worksheet 2.1 Silly Glasses on page 187 in Appendix B, glue, stickers, and craft decorations

Preparation: Cut out a pair of glasses for each child in your class (see template).

Procedure:

1. Remind children of the importance of looking at one another in the eyes.

2. Tell the children that they are going to make something to help them remember how important eye contact is.

3. Have children make glasses.

4. Teacher makes pair for self.

5. If class as a whole is challenged on eye contact, the teacher should wear glasses when giving important instructions. Phase out the visual cue by not using the glasses, but pretending to put them on to help the children remember.

2.1C Eye Contact Tag   *Time:* 10–15 minutes

Purpose: This gross motor game is beneficial for the kinesthetic learner: kids who are more attentive.

Materials: Polyspots, sit-upons, or pieces of construction paper

Preparation: None

Procedure:

1. One child is "it."

2. All other children are on a spot.

3. The child who is "it" goes around the room trying to get the other children to look into his or her eyes.

4. The child who is "it" cannot touch or get too close. Remind children that this is a game where sweet words are to be used.

5. If the first child gets someone to look at her or him, that person is "it" as well, and both children go and get as many others as they can.

6. Play until there is only one "not it" child remaining. That child is "it" to start the next round.

7. When working with large groups of younger children, hoops can be used instead of spots to support the use of appropriate body space.

2.1D Friendship Cards—Using Appropriate Eye Contact for Interaction   *Time:* 10–15 minutes

Purpose: The friendship cards are used as a visual reminder for the children to reinforce the concept that has been taught.

Materials: Friendship Cards in Appendix A:

- Why We Look at Other People
- Why Other People Look at Us

Preparation: See directions in "How to Use This Book" on page 12.

Procedure: See directions in "How to Use This Book" on page 12.

Generalization and Consistency

- Use praise and behavior-specific feedback every time the children make appropriate eye contact to help them to identify what eye contact actually is.

L esson 2.2   **Looking to Talk**

Introduction/Overview

Many of the children we work with who have poor eye contact also have difficulty initiating interactions with other children. Sometimes they can even have the same difficulty with adults. What we have found is that is these children are not using eye contact as a verbal cue in communication.

Teaching Concepts

- Looking tells people that we are talking to them.
- Looking tells people how we feel about what we are saying.
- Looking tells people when we are done talking and that it is their turn to talk.

Attitudinal Approach

- It is our own responsibility to make sure we are heard and other people are listening.
- If children are not making eye contact with a person, then they are not talking to that person.

Lesson Objectives

- Children will make eye contact when requesting something from an adult or peer.
- Children will make eye contact when they are telling stories and sharing information with adults and peers.

Lesson Introduction

Concept Map—Looking to Talk

Have children develop a concept map (see Figure 2.1) to refer to by asking leading questions. Use the directions found on page 11 in the "How to Use This Book" section. *Time:* 10–15 minutes.

Suggested Questions

- What part of our body do we look at when we are talking? (Face)
- What part of the face do we look at? (Eyes)
- Why do we look at the eyes when we are talking? (See and show emotions, get people's attention, so people know we are talking to them, helps us to be heard, so people can see what we need)

Figure 2.1 Looking to Talk Concept Map

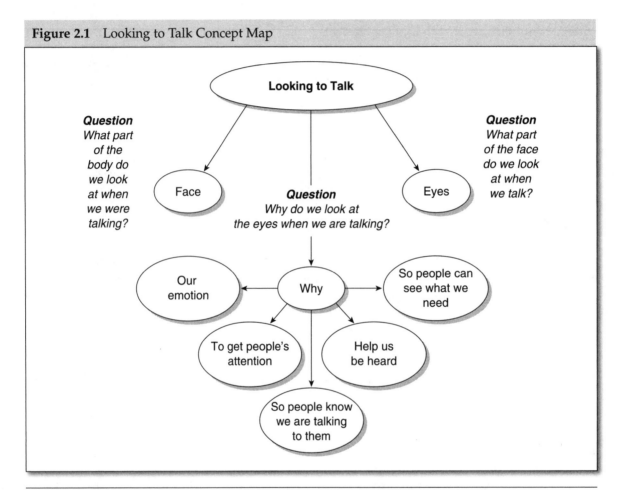

Activities

2.2A "Why We Look" Poster
Time: 15–20 minutes

Purpose: Many children learn from lists and visual references hung in the classroom. This will be a fun way to create something that is meaningful and visually interesting that can be referenced for the rest of the school year.

Materials: Poster, "Eye Coloring" template found in Appendix B

Preparation: Re-create the list of why we look at others when we talk to others on a poster. Make a copy of eyes for each child in class.

Procedure:

1. Review the list of why we look when we talk.

2. Have children color in the eyes and cut out to add to poster.

2.2B Hi—Howdy—Hello   *Time:* 5–10 minutes

Purpose: This game is a great way to help children work on attending to who is making eye contact with them. It also helps the sequencing skills needed for following a group discussion.

Materials: None

Preparation: None

Procedure:

1. The object of the game is to keep the conversation going as long as you can.

2. The conversation has only three words: "Hi," Howdy," or "Hello."

3. The first child says "Hi" to someone, and then that child will say "Howdy" or "Hello" to the next child. The children need to use eye contact to indicate who should go next.

4. Sit children in circle.

5. Have one child start.

6. If a child misses his or her cue because he or she is not looking, or says one of the words but not with eye contact, then that child is out.

2.2C Talking Down the Lane   *Time:* 5–10 minutes

Purpose: This is another opportunity for children to practice saying things to others' eyes.

Materials: None

Preparation: None

Procedure:

1. Someone picks a funny phrase for the whole group to use.

2. Each child takes a turn saying the funny phrase to another child in the group.

3. Each child needs to pay attention to the eye contact the other children are making with others in the class, so that she or he knows when it is her or his turn.

4. If a child misses a cue because he or she is not looking or says one of the words without eye contact, then that child is out.

5. When a child is out, she or he must think of the next silly phrase.

2.2D Name Ball

Time: 5–10 minutes

Purpose: To increase eye contact by using the game to strengthen the use of eye contact while using someone's name to get his or her attention.

Materials: Tennis ball or small rubber ball

Preparation: None

Procedure:

1. Have children sit in a circle on top of their desks.

2. The object of the game is to cue the person you are going to throw the ball to by making direct, sustained eye contact with him or her.

3. Explain that the person throwing the ball must be sure that the person she or he wants to throw to is looking directly at her or him.

4. Either have the group work as a team with the goal of playing for 2 minutes with the least number of drops, or play so that if the ball drops, the person throwing the ball is out. Creating a goal or challenge will cause the children to take more care in ensuring the person catching is looking and attending.

5. After the first round, challenge the group to do it again with fewer drops.

2.2E "What Do I Mean?" Charades

Time: 10–15 minutes

Purpose: To begin or expand the children's understanding of the importance of looking at people to be able to recognize their emotions when interacting with them

Materials: Social Phrases Flashcards (page 190) and Emotion Flashcards (page 206) in Appendix B

Preparation: Use two sets of cards, one with emotions and the other with phrases.

Procedure:

1. Put the group in pairs or choose a volunteer to be the first to participate.

2. Have one of the children pick a card from each set.

3. Ask that child to read the phrase and use the appropriate emotion in his or her voice and face.

4. Have the other child, or remainder of the group, guess the emotion.

5. To expand on the activity, have the child first read the phrase aloud facing away from the other child or group, and then read it again while facing the others.

2.2F Friendship Cards—Using Appropriate Eye Contact for Interaction

Time: 5–10 minutes

Purpose: The friendship cards are used as a visual reminder for the children to reinforce the concept that has been taught.

Materials: Friendship Cards in Appendix A:

- Where We Look When We Are Talking
- Why We Look at the Eyes When We Are Talking

Preparation: See directions in "How to Use This Book" on page 12.

Procedure: See directions in "How to Use This Book" on page 12.

Generalization and Consistency

To expand eye contact, do the following:

- Hold all objects of interest up to face and near eyes.
- Use gestures, such as pointing to nose while talking, to cue the children about eye contact when talking.
- Use the list of why we look at people to give behavior-specific feedback to children on their eye contact when talking.
- Request eye contact when the children are making statements or requesting objects.
- Request eye contact from the children at every opportunity. Use visual prompts such as pointing to your eyes.
- If children ask questions or request something without eye contact, either do not respond until they look at you or tell them you cannot hear what they are saying unless they are looking at you.
- "Are you asking/talking to me or are you asking/talking to (what the children are looking at)?"
- Use the list of why we look to give behavior-specific feedback to children on their eye contact.

 esson 2.3

Looking to Listen

Introduction/Overview

All children with attention issues will improve their ability to focus if their eye contact is strengthened and supported in the classroom. If the children are not visually attending, it is too easy for their minds to wander and for them to get fragmented and disjointed information. Focused eye contact can also aid those with auditory processing issues. On the other side of the interaction, the speaker will have difficulty determining if the child is still listening. Adults can react by assuming the child is being defiant or unfocused, and other children can think the child is uninterested in playing.

Teaching Concepts

- Looking is listening.
- We need to be looking at those with whom we are speaking so they know we are listening. If we look away, they will think we are not listening.
- We look at people for the entire time they are talking so we hear every word they say.
- We need to do three things to listen: look (make eye contact), hear (understand), and think (remember).
- Wait your turn to speak.
- We listen to understand our friends.

Attitudinal Approach

- What others want to say is interesting.
- This is a skill to be learned, not an action to be forced.
- Eye contact is the key to listening and showing that you are listening to others.
- Listening is very difficult in visually and auditorily challenging situations.
- Visual and tactical supports should be used to help with listening.

Lesson Objectives

- Children will hold eye contact with their peers and with adults for directions.
- Children will hold eye contact with their peers and adults for stories and discussion.
- Children will track from speaker to speaker in group discussion.
- Children will make sustained eye contact when listening to an adult.
- Children will make sustained eye contact when listening to other children.
- Children's attention and eye contact will move from one speaker to another.
- Children will follow multistep directions for a game.
- Children will list reasons why listening is important in relationships.
- Children will use responsive facial expressions to show they are listening.

Lesson Introduction

Concept Map—Looking to Listen

Have children develop a concept map (see Figure 2.2) to refer to by asking leading questions. Use the directions found on page 11 in the "How to Use This Book" section. *Time:* 5–10 minutes.

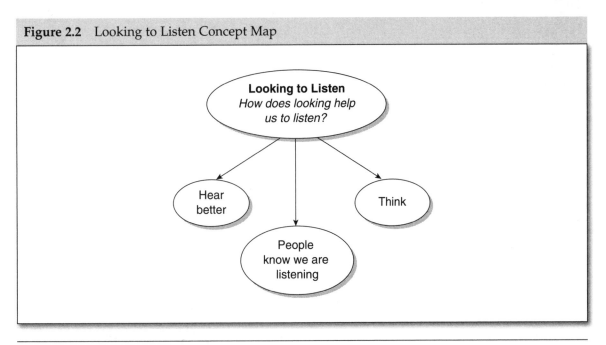

Figure 2.2 Looking to Listen Concept Map

Activities

2.3A Mirror Game

Time: 5–10 minutes

Purpose: This game is perfect for developing the duration of interactive eye contact. The success lies in the silliness. Also, the participants will encourage each other to hold eye contact.

Materials: None

Procedure:

1. Pair off the children and have them sit facing their partner.

2. In each pair, one child is the actor and the other is the mirror.

3. The actor moves his or her arms and makes different facial expressions.

4. The mirror must follow the actor exactly.

5. Remind actors that they can cue their mirror if she or he stops attending.

6. After a minute, have the actor and mirror switch roles. Keep switching back and forth, increasing the amount of time the children stay in a role.

2.3B Silent Simon Says

Time: 5–10 minutes

Purpose: This activity is key for children who have poor eye contact but have not been challenged on it, because they will attend enough to pick up most of the verbal directions. This will help give the child an experience that will illustrate how much can be missed when we are not looking to learn.

Materials: None

Procedure:

1. Each person takes a turn being Simon in a game of Simon Says.

2. Simon is not allowed to talk.

3. If someone misses a motion, he or she sits down.

4. For younger children, give a small verbal cue like "try/do this."

5. For older children, do action quickly and then put hands down. Let the children know they need to hold the motion.

6. For an extra challenge, also do two activities in a row, such as touch nose/stick out tongue.

2.3C Storytelling Game

Time: 10–15 minutes

Purpose: This game helps the children to see how much easier it is to hear and understand what people are saying when they are making eye contact.

Materials: None

Preparation: None

Procedure:

1. Either split the children into teams or have them play individually.

2. Facilitator tells a story with three specific details.

3. Children then raise their hands and tell what they remember from the story. Individuals or teams are given a point for each thing they remember.

4. Use visual cues, such as memory cards, that will help the children remember what the story was about in the first place (e.g., use a picture of a sneaker and tell a story of your favorite sneaker).

5. You can also divide the children into pairs and have them take turns telling a story or saying what they remember.

2.3D Guess a Doodle

Time: 10–20 minutes

Purpose: Children need to make eye contact to attend to the clues in order to guess the answer.

Materials: Guess a Doodle by Pressman Toy Co., or "Picture Flashcards" (page 179) in Appendix B

Preparation: Cut quarter-page pieces of scrap paper so each child has 5 to 10.

Procedure:

1. Someone is the describer, and the rest of the children are the artists.

2. The person describing picks a card and gives clues for the others to guess what is on the card.

3. The others do not call out, but rather draw a picture of what they think the card might show.

4. After all clues are given, all the children share their pictures to see who was right.

2.3E Friendship Cards—Using Appropriate Eye Contact for Interaction

Time: 10–15 minutes

Purpose: The friendship cards are used as a visual reminder for the children to reinforce the concept that has been taught.

Materials: Friendship Card in Appendix A: How Looking Helps Us to Listen

Preparation: See directions in "How to Use This Book" on page 12.

Procedure: See directions in "How to Use This Book" on page 12.

Generalization and Consistency

- Minimize the visual and auditory distractions when requesting the child's listening and attention. This will allow the children to focus on and process what is being said. (Sidebar conversation or other adults talking on the side will challenge the children's ability to hear, let alone listen.)
- Request eye contact when the children are making statements or asking for objects.
- Hold all objects of interest up to face and near eyes.
- Use gestures, such as pointing to nose while talking, to cue the children about eye contact when listening.
- If you lose the children's eye contact during directions or answering questions, stop talking until the children's eye contact comes back to you.
- Help children lengthen the duration of listening by giving directions or answering questions slowly so they need to hold eye contact.
- "Keep looking at my eyes so you hear all the directions (or story, or what I have to say)."
- "Help your friends talk by quietly looking while they talk."

Lesson 2.4

Looking to Learn

Introduction/Overview

The purpose of this lesson is to help the child develop a sense of visual acuity. Many children with social challenges are poor at perceiving visual details. This lesson helps them to search with their eyes in a way that will help them see the different social cues of others and learn from them. Children who have trouble with this lesson should be given extra support on clueing in to the details.

Teaching Concepts

- We use our eyes to find clues in the environment.
- We look for clues about our friends and their wants and needs.
- If we miss the clues, we can pick the wrong response.

Attitudinal Approach

- This is a learned behavior, and even children in higher grades might not have learned this skill.
- If this is a challenge for the children, they will need more than this lesson to master the skill.
- This has nothing to do with sight or needing glasses.

Lesson Objectives

- Children will be able to find an object in a visually distracting picture.
- Children will find an object in a visually distracting room.
- Children will identify someone's attitude or emotional state by observing non-verbal cues.
- Children will identify someone's intention by observing nonverbal cues.

Lesson Introduction

Concept Map—Looking to Learn

Have children develop a concept map (see Figure 2.3) to refer to by asking leading questions. Use the directions found on page 11 in the "How to Use This Book" section. *Time:* 10–15 minutes.

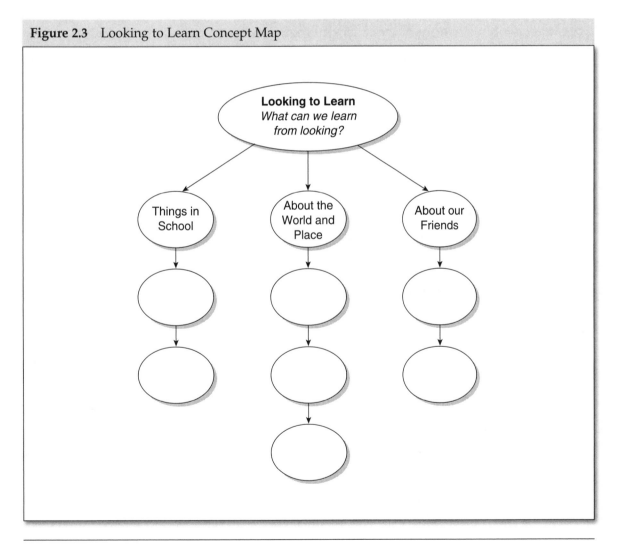

Figure 2.3 Looking to Learn Concept Map

Activities

2.4A Doggy, Where Is Your Bone?

Time: 10–15 minutes

Purpose: The children will use their eyes to look for an item in a room and concentrate on the looking process.

Materials: An eraser or item to hide

Preparation: None

Procedure:

1. One child plays the part of the dog.

2. He or she sits in front of the other children with his or her back to the group.

3. The item (the bone) is put under her or his chair.

4. While the "dog" is turned around with his or her eyes closed, pick someone to sneak up and steal the bone and hide it somewhere on his or her person.

5. Then everyone sings,

   "Doggy, doggy where is your bone? Somebody's stolen it from your home. Guess who it might be."

6. Then the dog has three chances to guess who took the bone.

7. Sometimes the bone can be left under the dog's chair.

8. If the dog guesses right, he or she can do it again.

9. If the dog is wrong, the person who had the bone is now the dog.

2.4B I Spy

Time: 15–25 minutes

(This activity can be broken up into two sessions if attention is an issue.)

Purpose: This activity is a fun way to give children an opportunity to use eye contact and descriptive words to listen and learn.

Materials: I Spy by Walter Wick (photographs), Jean Marzolo (riddles), and Carol Devine Carson (design); poster paper; stickers; stamps; crayons; markers; and magazine pictures used for collages

Preparation: Have supplies ready to make the poster.

Procedure:

1. Read *I Spy*.

2. Make "I Spy" poster or individual collages using stickers, magazine photos, or pictures drawn by the children.

3. Have each child lead an "I Spy" by giving clues for the other children to find the picture he or she is looking at. Prompt eye contact both on the picture and between children.

2.4C Friendship Cards—Using Appropriate Eye Contact for Interaction

Time: 10–15 minutes

Purpose: The friendship cards are used as a visual reminder for the children to reinforce the concept that has been taught.

Materials: Friendship Card in Appendix A: What We Learn From Looking

Preparation: See directions in "How to Use This Book" on page 12.

Procedure: See directions in "How to Use This Book" on page 12.

Generalization and Consistency

- Give the children verbal prompts for all the times they need to be attentive by starting your address with, "Everyone look at my eyes so you can hear all the directions."
- Use visual prompts to assist language processing, such as holding a finger up for each direction to help the children to remember.
- Use redirection phrases such as "Remember the directions," "Think about what you should be doing now," and "Think about the direction I just gave."
- Give children more opportunities to look for and retrieve the materials they need.
- Give children more specific direction when sending them to find something on their own.
- Give children more visual supports, such as writing lists of directions or placing reminder cards on their desks, to help them retain direction during the day.
- Use other nonverbal forms of communication, such as facial expression, gestures, and fluctuation of tone or volume, to keep children's eye contact.
- Make sure the children are given enough time to answer questions and respond. (Some adults restate questions or even repeat the question after waiting a short amount of time. We need to factor in the possibility that some children may need more time to process what was just said to them and then answer. Practice waiting twice the time for the children to answer so they have more opportunity to process the first statement before we give them another to deal with.)

Lesson 2.5

Interest in Others

Introduction/Overview

This lesson is an opportunity for children to understand the importance of having others in their lives. The belief that all children want to interact is an incomplete idea. It is very possible that there are children you are working with who do not see the importance of other people. Traditionally, the concentration would be on why the children "feel" this way about others. In this section, we are concentrating on helping children understand the benefit, and develop the concept, of having others in their lives. This is also an opportunity for the teacher to get a sense of what may be challenging for each individual child when he or she is interacting.

Teaching Concepts

- Other people are fun and great to spend time with.
- Even if it may be difficult to interact with others, it has great benefits.

Attitudinal Approach

- We love being with others, and we want to make more opportunities to spend time with others.
- We are nonjudgmental of those children who will have difficulty with this concept.
- We believe that all children have the ability to develop these skills.

Lesson Objectives

- Children will initiate play with other children.
- Children will choose activities that include others over solitary activities.
- Children will engage in reciprocal activities with another child.
- Children will list the things that are positive about others and about spending time with others.

Lesson Introduction

Brainstorm for Key Concepts

Have children develop lists to refer to by asking specific questions. Use the directions found on page 11 in the "How to Use This Book" section. *Time:* 5–10 minutes.

- What are the games and activities we do with others?
- What do we talk to other people about?
- How do others help us?
- Why do we have friends?

Activities

2.5A Name Ball

Time: 10–15 minutes

Purpose: This activity is just like the game of Silent Ball, but with an emphasis on eye contact and names. We really need to make the connection for children that addressing someone must include eye contact.

Materials: Small ball, polyspots and sit-upons (if needed), or desks

Preparation: None

Procedure:

1. Set up spots in a circle for children to sit on or have all the children put them in a circle for you.

2. When all children are sitting, designate someone to be the starter.

3. The child needs to say the name of another child, look at that child, and then throw the ball to that child.

4. If the person throwing does not look at the person he or she is throwing to, then the thrower is out. If the person catching does not catch the ball, the catcher is out.

2.5B Paper Dolls

Time: 15–20 minutes

Purpose: The purpose of this activity is to have children express the qualities they like in others. It will help them to bring the things they like about others to the forefront of their minds before they get into the deeper concepts.

Materials: Worksheet 4.2 Paper Doll on page 199 in Appendix B, markers, and crayons

Preparation: Cut out a paper doll for each child.

Procedure:

1. Use the list generated from brainstorming to help children think of ideas of things to do with friends and talk to friends about.

2. Have children draw a picture of someone who is their friend or someone they would like to be their friend.

3. Have children draw symbols or write words on the back of the doll, explaining the things they do and talk about with friends.

2.5C Who's It Going to Be?

Time: 10–15 minutes

Purpose: This activity allows the children to think of different people to do fun activities with so they will begin to see the benefits of interacting with these people.

Materials: Worksheet 2.3 Who's It Going to Be? on page 189 in Appendix B

Preparation: None

Procedure:

1. Have children in the group fill out the worksheet, encouraging them to think of different people for each activity listed.

2. After they have completed the sheet, have the children share their answers with the group.

2.5D Friendship Cards—Using Appropriate Eye Contact for Interaction

Time: 10–15 minutes

Purpose: The friendship cards are used as a visual reminder for the children to reinforce the concept that has been taught.

Materials: Friendship Cards in Appendix A:

- What We Do With Others
- Why We Have Friends

Preparation: See directions in "How to Use This Book" on page 12.

Procedure: See directions in "How to Use This Book" on page 12.

Generalization and Consistency

- Spend time following the children's lead in play and expressing your interest and enjoyment of the things they find fun. Add on to games a piece at a time and see if the children will attempt the things that you try. Cheer their exploration of new play each time they try something they observe.
- If children are requesting a toy for themselves, ask them who they are going to use it with or prompt them to go ask a particular child.
- Celebrate every attempt and accomplishment the children make to initiate activity with others.

Social Skills for Interacting With Friends

The concept of friendship should constantly be discussed with children, as children benefit from learning the strategies needed to be a "good" friend to others. This lesson introduces the basic concepts necessary to having successful friendships. Often, children may not have the desire to have friends; sometimes friends are just too challenging and it is easier to play alone. We have to make friendship fun or the children will not see the benefit of trying. By teaching children phrases and actions that will increase their success during play, the play becomes more fun, and children are then willing to try harder to build relationships with peers. The following lessons teach simplistic skills to the children that will help them make playing more fun.

SOCIAL GOALS

- Child will engage in unstructured interactive play with similar toys with other children.
- Child will invite a peer to play.
- Child will join another child or group of children when asked to play a game or participate in an activity.
- Child will use "sweet" language to communicate with others.
- Child will follow a play theme until game or activity is finished.
- Child will use show good sportsmanship in a game by cheering on a peer.

Lesson 3.1

Fun With Friends

Introduction/Overview

The purpose of this lesson is to begin to lay out the basic concepts of the Wanna Play Program. From this basic social structure, we have branched out into all of the different concepts we use. We use the terms "sweet words" and "kind words" interchangeability. "Sweet words" is geared toward younger children who still interact through a gross motor and dramatic play. "Kind words" is geared toward older elementary children who spend less of their time interacting through play. Others have also used "polite words" or even "friendly words." The key is to remain consistent in the phrase you adopt so children are hearing the same thing over again. Each of the other lessons has similar interchangeable terms.

The Wanna Play Program is developed to build on itself with each concept supporting the next. In each consecutive lesson, the attitudes and objectives need to be reviewed. Therefore, in this lesson and all others, eye contact and interaction need to be continually reinforced on a daily basis.

Teaching Concepts

- Being a friend has different components.
- Having friends and being friends are important in our lives.
- It is important to choose positive words and actions every time you play and interact with others.
- Everyone needs to have the skills to interact with others in a positive way.

Attitudinal Approach

- Play is fun, and we believe you can do it.
- Even though this may be hard for children with disassociative disorders, we still need to teach it until they learn it because they can learn it.

Lesson Objectives

- Children will be introduced to the beginning concepts of play that are coming up in the next lessons.
- Children will be introduced to the idea that play is an activity that involves others.

Lesson Introduction

Brainstorm for Key Concepts

Have children develop lists to refer to by asking specific questions. Use the directions found on page 11 in the "How to Use This Book" section. *Time:* 10–15 minutes.

- Who are your friends? Allow children to include parents, cousins, and other family members.
- What do we do with friends?
- Why do we have friend and other people in our lives?
- What do you do to be a good friend? Give examples of traits that the children can use if they are stuck. Also, use the list of specific people to help them come up with adjectives.

Activities

3.1A Friendship Poster

Time: 15–20 minutes

Purpose: This activity helps the children make a visual reminder of who their friends are and things they like to do with friends.

Materials: Large paper for poster, 8½ × 11 paper, markers or crayons, glue sticks, construction paper (optional)

Preparation: None

Procedure:

1. Have children draw a picture of themselves and a friend doing something together. If it is not clear what the picture is showing, ask the child who it is and what they are doing, and then label the picture for them.

2. The children can then cut out the picture and glue it on construction paper or directly on the poster.

3. Label the top of the poster "Fun With Friends."

3.1B Friendship Train

Time: 10–15 minutes

Purpose: The Friendship Train activity can be adapted to teach many different friend concepts. The questions asked to the children can be modified to fit the friend concept that is appropriate for the group or child.

Materials: Worksheet 3.1 Friendship Train on page 193 in Appendix B, crayons or markers.

Preparation: Make copies of coloring sheets and gather supplies.

Procedure:

1. Ask the children the friendship question that is appropriate for their age or level of concept development. Examples: "What do you like to do with your friends?" "Who are your friends?"

2. Otherwise, just list the names of the children and have it be a train of the friends in the class.

3. Either have the children write the answer on the train or write it for them.

4. The children can then color the train, cut out the train, and glue the train onto construction paper.

5. Photographs of the children can be added to their train if available.

6. Hang the train pictures around the room to help remind the children of who their friends are in the group.

 ## 3.1C Friendship Cards—Social Skills for Interacting With Friends

Time: 5–10 minutes

Purpose: The friendship cards are used as a visual reminder for the children to reinforce the concept that has been taught.

Materials: Friendship Card in Appendix A: What You Do to Be a Good Friend

Preparation: See directions in "How to Use This Book" on page 12.

Procedure: See directions in "How to Use This Book" on page 12.

Consistency and Generalization

- Pick a social situation (i.e., a birthday party) and have the children draw pictures of themselves at the event.
- If children are not doing representative drawing, have them color in pictures of children playing well together.
- Celebrate children's attempts to initiate play or join others in play activities.
- Ask open-ended questions about children's play experiences when you are not with them.
- Use the word *friend* whenever possible when describing peers together.

 # Lesson 3.2

Sweet Words/Kind Words

Introduction/Overview

This lesson addresses the importance of positive proactive speech, which we, for the sake of the children, refer to as "sweet words." As immature as the phrase may seem, we have attempted different phrases, and "sweet words" is the one children seem to remember the best over time. The phrase "sweet words" refers to both the language we choose to communicate with as well the tone of voice we adopt. For some groups, whining, grumpy, or brusque tones of voice are not an issue. However, we suggest helping children identify what this sounds like when others use it and ways of avoiding using these tones.

Teaching Concepts

- The best way to communicate is with a positive affect.
- You get more of what you want if you stay calm and positive.
- The way we speak to people helps them to know what kind of person we are.
- Sweet/kind goes with any emotion.
- Sometimes being sweet is just being calm and nonjudgmental.
- Kind words are the best way to get what you want.
- People are more willing to help when you treat them kindly.
- Friends are more willing to be with you if you are kind.
- People will know how you want to be treated.

Attitudinal Approach

- Use it or lose it: If we do not model it consistently, the children will not use the positive language.
- Make it big enough to notice: Many children need us to overemphasize the positive tones and language in order for them to understand the difference between what we are saying and what they are using.

Lesson Objectives

- Children will identify positive language and phrases that they can use in both everyday situations as well as conflict situations with their peers.
- Children will use sweet/kind words when communicating with others.

Lesson Introduction

Brainstorm for Key Concepts

Have children develop lists to refer to by asking specific questions. Use the directions found on page 11 in the "How to Use This Book" section. *Time:* 10–15 minutes.

- What are sweet/kind words?
- Brainstorm a list of the sweet words that the children know. Examples: "Please," "Thank you," "You're welcome," "Sorry," "May I . . . ?" "Will you . . . ?"
- Whom would we use our sweet words with?
- Why do we use sweet words and a sweet voice with our friends?

Activities

3.2A Sweet Words Mobile

Time: 5–10 minutes

Purpose: Make a mobile of the words children use to be sweet/kind. This is a good opportunity to test the retention of the students.

Materials: Paper for writing words, hole punch, string, paper plates or hangers

Preparation: Copy words for children to color in and cut out.

Procedure:

1. Use children's brainstormed sweet words to make bubble letter words.
2. Have children color in the words and cut out the letters.
3. Punch holes in the top of letters.
4. Make a separate mobile for each word.
5. Hang letters from a paper plate or hanger.

3.2B Making Phrases Sweeter

Time: 5–10 minutes

Purpose: Analyze the phrases that we use and hear and find out if they are "sweet words" and if they can be improved on.

Materials: Posters/easel paper, markers or crayons

Preparation: Make a list of words/phrases used by the children or by their favorite characters and cartoons. Write them out on one poster for children. Use ones the children have used or ones that can be found in the current culture, including popular cartoon characters.

Procedure:

1. Show children and read the list of words and phrases.
2. Have children identify which are "sweet words" and which are not.
3. As a class or in small groups, have the children rephrase the words to make them "sweet words."

3.2C Role-Play With Friends

Time: 10–15 minutes

Purpose: Opportunity to act out and practice the social skills taught

Materials: Situation Flashcards on page 196 in Appendix B, paper bags for puppets, markers or crayons

Preparation: Cut out flashcards. Have children make paper bag puppets of themselves.

Procedure:

1. Using situation cards, decide the sweet words you need.

2. Have children volunteer to role-play using the situation cards provided. Each child takes a turn playing a character and playing herself or himself.

3. Have the audience reflect and brainstorm other thing that could have been said.

 ## 3.2D Drawing With Limited Materials   *Time:* 10–15 minutes

Purpose: Creates a need to communicate and request things using sweet words

Materials: Crayons/markers, large white paper

Preparation: Remind children about sweet words and how we use them when we are working together. Write sweet words from brainstorm list in bubble letters on the large white paper.

Procedure:

1. Create a poster of some of the sweet words the children have brainstormed, using bubble letters for the children to fill in.

2. Have limited markers/crayons on the table to encourage the children to have to request from one another.

 ## 3.2E Topple by Pressman Toys   *Time:* See game rules.

Purpose: This is a great game to use to help children use sweet words in the context of turn taking. There is a fine motor challenge imbedded in the game that needs to be kept in mind.

Materials: See game.

Preparation: See game.

Procedure:

1. Play the game according to the rules of the game or have the children brainstorm new or additional rules first, write them down, and play by those rules.

2. Concentrate on the positive words used during the game.

3. Focus on pointing out how the children respond to friends during a game.

3.2F Mother, May I?

Time: 5–10 minutes

Purpose: The competition of these games will affect the attitude and verbal requesting of the participants.

Materials: None

Preparation: None

Procedure:

1. Line children up on one side of the room/playground.

2. Call each child at a time and let him or her request, using sweet words, to come closer to you.

3. The first person to reach the leader wins.

4. Give children behavior-specific feedback on how well they requested with sweet words.

3.2G Friendship Cards—Social Skills for Interacting With Friends

Time: 5–10 minutes

Purpose: The friendship cards are used as a visual reminder for the children to reinforce the concept that has been taught.

Materials: Friendship Cards in Appendix A:

- Sweet Words You Can Use
- Why We Use Sweet/Kind Words With Our Friends

Preparation: See directions in "How to Use This Book" on page 12.

Procedure: See directions in "How to Use This Book" on page 12.

Generalization and Consistency

Developing a Positive Affect

- These are the terms used when discussing positive behavior with the child:
  - Sweet words/kind words—polite language
  - Sweet voice/kind voice—kind tone of voice

- Celebrate every attempt children make to use positive proactive language.
- Prompt sweet/kind words and voice for children. Initially give the phrases or model the voice that is more positive. Transition to just asking the child to try it again.
- When the children choose to whine, complain, or pout as a means of responding to not getting their way, little to no emotional response should be given. Tell them you do not understand them when they choose these behaviors. Explain what their choices are, how to accept what is being offered, and how to attempt a new, positive way to get what they want or continue to be unhappy. The choice is up to them. Then walk away.
- Use these phrases in everyday activity to help remind children to use sweet/kind words:
  - "Say it with your sweet/kind words."
  - "Say it again with a sweet/kind voice."
  - "Say it again with a calm voice."

- Use behavior-specific feedback to help children see how and when they are using this type of communication.
  - "Thank you for asking with sweet/kind words."
  - "I appreciate your using sweet/kind words."
  - "Those sweet/kind words really make me want to help you."
  - "Because you used your sweet/kind words, your friends want to play with/help you."

Lesson 3.3 — Safe Body/Body Safety

Introduction/Overview

Children's ability to have an awareness of their body space can be challenged by sensory needs that are not even diagnosed. Children frequently are not cognitive of how close they are to another person. Also, children with social challenges use physical actions to attempt to interact when they do not know what else to do; physical humor is easy to use and can get more attention from peers. All of the aforementioned possibilities impede the children's ability to choose appropriate body actions. The following activities will begin to teach children how to safely use their body.

Teaching Concepts

- Safety is the only way to be friendly.
- A friend's safety is more important than humor.
- Using our words, not our bodies, helps to get us what we want.
- We need to use our eyes to see where our bodies are.
- You need to practice controlling your impulses.
- Use toys in a safe way.

Attitudinal Approach

- Acts of physical force are used when we do not have the words to use.
- Children need to be taught to use words instead of being punished for actions.
- Children need to be shown how to safely use their bodies.

Lesson Objectives

- Children will respect the personal space of peers and adults.
- Children will ask before they touch, hug, or hold the hand of a peer or adult.
- Children will begin a conversation with a peer or adult, instead of hugging them to begin a social interaction.
- Children will use appropriate levels of movement and energy for different activities and environments.

Lesson Introduction

Brainstorm for Key Concepts

Have children develop lists to refer to by asking specific questions. Use the directions found on page 11 in the "How to Use This Book" section. *Time:* 10–15 minutes.

- Why do we keep our body safe?
- Why do we keep our friend's body safe?
- How do we use our hands and have a safe body?
    - Gentle hands versus hitting hands
    - Keep hands to ourselves versus hands on our friends
- How do we use our feet and have a safe body?
    - Walking feet versus running feet
    - Keep feet to ourselves versus putting our feet on our friends
- Do we sit next to our friends or on top of our friends?
- Do we stand too close or keep a safe distance?
    - If children use "don'ts" (don't hit), change the don'ts into "dos." Children need to learn what to do. They know what not to do.

Activities

3.3A Making Safe Bodies

Time: 10–15 minutes

Purpose: Help teach children what to do by giving them a visual representation of what to do.

Materials: Worksheet 3.2 Safe Body on page 194 in Appendix B, markers or crayons

Preparation: Make copies of the body outlines.

Procedure:

1. Have the children color a body and make it into a friend by naming it.

2. Help the children name each body part, along with the appropriate safe action that was brainstormed in the lesson introduction.

3. Label the body parts for them.

4. Hang the body outlines in the room as visual aids, and use them to remind the children of safe body choices.

3.3B Musical Islands   *Time:* 5–10 minutes

Purpose: Continue to increase the children's awareness of where their body is in relation to others.

Materials: Polyspots, music

Preparation: None

Procedure:

1. Place polyspots on the floor and have the children stand around them.
2. Play music and have the children dance around the spots.
3. When the music stops, have each child jump onto a spot.
4. Before each round, remove one or two spots.
5. When there are fewer spots than children, the children are to begin to share spots. Remind the children about keeping their friends' bodies safe when they are on the spots.
6. The goal is for the children to place one foot all on one spot at the end, keeping a check on their bodies.
7. Continue to increase the children's awareness of where their body is in relation to others.

3.3C Safe Body Puzzle   *Time:* 5–10 minutes

Purpose: Another activity to help teach children what to do by giving them a visual representation of what to do

Materials: Worksheets 3.2 (Safe Body) on page 194 and 3.3 (Safe Body Clothes) on page 195 in Appendix B, markers, glue

Preparation: Make copies of the body outlines and cutout clothes (decide if you want to have the children cut out the clothes or if you should cut them out before giving them to the children).

Procedure:

1. Have each child make the body into a friend by naming it.

2. Help the children name each body part with the safe body activity. Refer to the brainstorming that has been done in previous lessons.

3. Label the body parts for them. Write the safe body parts on the clothes so the children can glue them onto their safe body.

4. Children can then color in the rest of the body.

5. Hang finished body outlines in the room as visual aids, and use them to remind the children of safe body choices.

3.3D Foot Loose by Interactive Playthings

Time: **See game rules.**

Purpose: Increases the children's awareness of how their body moves and how to switch from one movement to another.

Materials: See game.

Preparation: See game.

Procedure:

1. Play the game according to the rules of the game or have the children brainstorm new or additional rules first, write them down, and play by those rules.

2. Help the children build awareness of how much space they will need around their body before they do the exercise.

3. Point out the different body movements during each exercise.

3.3E Balloon Keep Up

Time: 5–10 minutes

Purpose: To build the children's awareness of where their body is in relation to others

Materials: Blown-up balloons

Preparation: None

Procedure:

1. Have children stand in a group in a large space.

2. The objective of the game is to keep tapping the balloon into the air without letting it drop on the ground.

3. Remind children that they need to stay on their feet and keep their friends' bodies safe.

4. Use the brainstormed list again to remind them what body safety is.

5. Continue to increase the children's awareness of where their body is in relation to others.

 ## 3.3F Parachute Keep Up

Time: 5–10 minutes

Purpose: Continue to increase the children's awareness of where their body is in relation to others. The activity also helps children begin to work as a group and observe others' movements in order to move with them.

Materials: Parachute, beanbag or small stuffed animal to toss in the air

Preparation: None

Procedure:

1. Have children stand in a circle and hold one or two handles of the parachute depending on its size.

2. Put the beanbag or stuffed animal in the center of the parachute.

3. The objective is to have all the children throw the beanbag or stuffed animal into the air in one motion and then catch it.

4. Count to see how many times you can catch it as a group.

5. When it drops, try again, and try to break your score as a group.

 ## 3.3G Friendship Cards—Social Skills for Interacting With Friends

Time: 5–10 minutes

Purpose: The friendship cards are used as a visual reminder for the children to reinforce the concept that has been taught.

Materials: Friendship Cards in Appendix A:

- Why We Keep Our Bodies Safe
- Why We Keep Our Friends' Bodies Safe

- How We Use Our Hands/Feet
- How We Use Our Bodies

Preparation: See directions in "How to Use This Book" on page 12.

Procedure: See directions in "How to Use This Book" on page 12.

Generalization and Consistency

- Giving the children suggestions of sensory intervention during moments of high challenge aids them in resolution.
- When children are not being safe, refer them to the friendship cards or the brainstorm list. Point out that what they are doing now is not safe, and have them tell what the appropriate action should be.
- Bring children back to the setting where they were not being safe and walk them through it, using the appropriate action, so they can have the experiential memory of the action being successful.
- If the children continue to use unsafe body behavior, they have chosen to move away from the activity.
  - Tell them they need to move away.
  - Remind them that they need to be safe.
  - Offer an appropriate behavior. Example: hold hands or sit next to you.

Lesson 3.4   **Playing Together**

Introduction/Overview

The goal of this lesson is to help the children learn all the things they need to remember to respect their friends and the toys during play and still have fun. The term *share* is constantly used to teach children to have successful interactions during play. Sharing is a conceptual idea, lacking definitive, clear time components. Children will more easily learn this idea by the facilitator using the phrase "take turns." Taking turns has a defined beginning and end and allows the person facilitating to give countdowns to warn the children about their turn. Children should also be given the choice of whether or not to bring out their own toys to share. It is all right to keep special toys for themselves. Before the play begins, you should explain to the children that if they bring out the toy or bring the toy to school, they will need to take turns with it. If they do not want to take turns, then they can leave the toy at home.

Teaching Concepts

- Respect others' creations and toys.
- Everyone has a right to keep their things safe.
- We show our friends we care by taking care of their things.
- Respect how others choose to play.

- We only add to someone's creation or game when invited.
- Our friends may disagree with us and that's OK.
- Everyone has the right to have fun.
- Everyone has the right to play their way.

Attitudinal Approach

- Not all choices children make during play seem fair to us or other children.
- When children are having fun, they may need positive reminders to make the best choices.

Lesson Objectives

- Children will physically show appreciation of others by including others and taking turns.
- Children will choose to play a friend's game or finish an activity that a friend wants to finish.
- Children will teach a friend to play a game.
- Children will try a new game to have fun.
- Children will attempt to join another child or group of children in play.

Lesson Introduction

Concept Map—What Do We Need to Do to Play Together and Have Fun?

Have children develop a concept map (see Figure 3.1) to refer to by asking leading questions. Use the directions found on page 11 in the "How to Use This Book" section. *Time:* 10–15 minutes.

Figure 3.1 What Do We Need to Do to Play Together and Have Fun Concept Map

Activities

3.4A Centers

Time: 15–20 minutes

Purpose: Providing the children the opportunity to participate in this activity allows them to try new activities and interact with other children participating in the activity.

Materials: Select toys/games that are age-appropriate and offer the children a chance to interact while they play. Buckets of cars and Legos are usually great ideas, along with card games or toys with a limited number of pieces.

Preparation: Arrange the toys/games in separate areas with enough space for the children to comfortably play.

Procedure:

1. Group the children in equal numbers, considering the dynamic and personalities of the group. Choose the dynamic of the group thinking about how much social challenge specific children can handle.

2. Explain that there will be a certain amount of time with each toy or game, and then you will switch. Try to give the children equal time with each center.

3. Prompt with a 2-minute countdown before switching.

4. During the playtime, facilitate from afar if possible. Look for opportunities to prompt what they have learned in the previous lessons. This is a great time to encourage the use of sweet/kind words, safe distance, and positive friendship skills.

5. Acknowledge all attempts by the children to interact positively with their friends.

3.4B Teach a Friend a Game

Time: 10–15 minutes

Purpose: This gives the children the opportunity to attempt beginning leadership skills and to manage their temptation to overuse their knowledge when explaining the directions.

Materials: Whatever game the children bring in. Help parents by giving guidelines for an appropriate game. The game should be able to include "___" number of players, and the children should have played the game enough to be comfortable explaining it to others.

Preparation: None

Procedure:

1. Have the children take turns bringing in a game from home to teach their friends. If it is a group larger than four children, break into smaller groups and have one child from each group bring in a game.

2. Send a note home reminding parents and instructing them that the game should be one that the children can play easily. They do not need to provide any additional instruction.

3. Before the children begin teaching their friends to play, remind the group of the things they have learned about being good friends. Review briefly the concepts in this unit that would be beneficial in this situation and for the group.

4. Facilitate as needed. The intention is to have the children be as independent as possible. Let the children finish the explanation once, and then ask the group if they have any questions.

5. Let the children attempt to answer the questions first. If some additional support is needed, give a brief instruction or two and then let them begin playing. Again, facilitate as needed.

6. Reinforce the concept by congratulating the children for bringing the game to teach their friends.

7. If the children in the group need more visual support for following directions, write the directions in a list to be visible as the children play the game.

3.4C Building With Friends

Time: 5–10 minutes

Purpose: Construct a play environment that requires positive interactions to have fun

Materials: Blocks or Legos, a hoop or tape circle on the floor

Preparation: None

Procedure:

1. Divide children into groups of four or less.

2. Explain that they are to build a specific construction (based on children's common interest) within the area (hoop) with the blocks or Legos you give them.

3. Facilitate as needed with prompts and reminders for positive interactions and problem solving.

3.4D Friendship Cards—Social Skills for Interacting With Friends

Time: 5–10 minutes

Purpose: The friendship cards are used as a visual reminder for the children to reinforce the concept that has been taught.

Materials: Friendship Card in Appendix A: What We Do Together to Play and Have Fun

Preparation: See directions in "How to Use This Book" on page 12.

Procedure: See directions in "How to Use This Book" on page 12.

Generalization and Consistency

- Continue to strengthen the children's ability to take turns. Suggest trades, substituting a new toy, and time-sharing in a conflict situation.
- When the children choose not to play friendly, remind them that they have now made the choice not to play and need to move away from the game until the game is over.
- If the children are requesting a toy for themselves, ask them who they are going to play it with or prompt them to go to ask a particular child.
- Being a friend—this means following directions, using a kind attitude, letting someone take a turn by himself or herself, keeping the game together when it needs to be, and coming to agreements.
- This is the time to set the rule in the classroom that choosing not to play friendly is choosing not to play.

UNIT 4

Appropriate Body Behavior

In many situations when a child is having difficulty making friends or behaving appropriately in a social setting, the problem is rooted in the child's body awareness and sensory regulation. Many children have the interest and desire to interact with others but have difficultly doing so because they are unaware of the appropriate way to behave and use their bodies.

SOCIAL GOALS

- Child will respect personal space of peers and adults by standing at appropriate distances during interaction.
- Child will use sensory suggestions when prompted by an adult or, when needed, without prompting.
- Child will ask before touching, hugging, or holding the hand of a peer or adult.
- Child will initiate a conversation or social interaction with a peer or adult with appropriate physical contact.
- Child will use appropriate levels of movement and energy for different activities and environments.

Lesson 4.1

Introduction to
Body Awareness

Introduction/Overview

The main purpose of this lesson is to review the safe body concepts that were introduced in Unit 3: Social Skills for Interacting With Friends. We want the children to build on the concepts that they have learned in previous lessons and to expanding their understanding that social skills do not exist in a vacuum but are interconnected. Reintroducing the body safety concepts will help the children establish the foundation of social interaction. We can then build on the concept of interaction and introduce the next level of social complexity.

Teaching Concepts

- We need to have a safe body when playing with our friends.
- We need to move at certain speeds in different situations to help keep our friends safe.
- People want to spend more time with us when we keep our bodies clean and dressed.

Attitudinal Approach

- Certain activities in this lesson, if not performed with care, can damage the children's body image, so we must always choose our words carefully.
- Being comfortable and positive when talking about sensitive issues will help children.

Lesson Objective

- Child will be introduced to the concepts of appropriate body.

Lesson Introduction

Brainstorm for Key Concepts

Have children develop lists to refer to by asking specific questions. Use the directions found on page 11 in the "How to Use This Book" section. *Time:* 10–15 minutes.

- Define "having an appropriate body."
- What do we do to use a safe body?

Activities

4.1A Body Outline Poster   *Time:* 15–20 minutes

Purpose: This is a fun activity to introduce the unit. It gives the children some self-expression. It also gives the adult a look into the children's self-image and body concept.

Materials: Large roll of paper or butcher paper, markers/crayons, lots of space

Preparation: Cut a long piece of paper for each child off of the roll.

Procedure:

1. Have children get into pairs.

2. Have one child lie on the floor and the other child trace the lying child onto the large paper. Then have the children switch so each child has an outline of his or her body.

3. Have the children make the bodies look like themselves. Instruct them to draw their face and the clothes they like to wear.

4. Have children write three or four words from the list of concept development onto the posters, above the pictures of their bodies.

5. For younger children, write the words and the terms from the concept development for them in bubble letters.

4.1B Mirror Game

Time: 5–10 minutes

Purpose: In this game, children are using their bodies in sync with another child. It gives the children the opportunity to have to regulate their movements in coordination with someone else. Even when they want to move fast, they need to follow the other child.

Materials: Polyspots or construction paper taped to the ground (optional)

Preparation: None

Procedure:

1. Have children face each other either sitting cross-legged.

2. Have the children decide who is the mirror.

3. Instruct the children that the child who is not the mirror will do certain things that the mirror needs to copy.

4. After some time, have the children stand (use spots to help kids stay in place if needed) and play again standing. Encourage the children to use their whole bodies.

4.1C Human Obstacle Course

Time: 10–15 minutes

Purpose: In this game, children form the obstacle course as well as go through it. Children will need to be careful of their friends and use appropriate behavior to get through the course correctly.

Materials: Open safe space, polyspots or construction paper taped to the ground or sit-upons, optional balls

Preparation: None

Procedure:

1. Tell the children that they will do another obstacle course, but this time they will *be* the obstacle course.

2. Split the children into two groups.

3. Have one group sit and wait and the other group find a spot for each child.

4. Go through the children and have them decide what obstacle they would like to be.

5. Make suggestions if a child has trouble coming up with ideas (tell him or her to be something people have to crawl under or something people need to jump over; children can use balls if they want to be human basket hoops).

6. Have the remaining children go through the course one at a time. Remind the children to use their bodies appropriately.

7. Switch groups and have the other children make a new course.

4.1D Hula Hoop

Time: 5–10 minutes

Purpose: This activity gives children a chance to move their bodies at different speeds and in different directions.

Materials: Hula hoops (one for each child), music that goes at different speeds (rock and roll to classical)

Preparation: Put the hula hoops on the ground spaced far enough apart that children will not bump into one another.

Procedure:

1. Have every child choose a hoop and sit in the middle of it.

2. Explain that the object of the game is to follow the music and direction the best you can.

3. Put one speed of music on and give movement direction to kids, such as
   a. Jump in and out
   b. Run around outside of hoop
   c. Run around inside the hoop
   d. Walk around with one foot inside and one foot outside

4. Try the same movements with a different speed of music.

4.1E Relay Race

Time: 10–15 minutes

Purpose: This gives the children the chance to use a multitude of skills. In this case, they will be asked to concentrate on using appropriate body movements to complete the tasks and keep everyone safe.

Materials: Spoons, golf balls, pom-pom balls, balloons

Preparation: Split the children into groups and set up the course.

Procedure:

1. Run relay races.
2. Each child needs to run down and back with the ball on the spoon without dropping the ball. If a child drops the ball, she or he has to start over.
3. Start with the heaviest ball (it will stay on the spoon the best).
4. With each race introduce a new ball or the balloon.
5. Remind the children they need to pay attention to their bodies and comment if someone becomes too crazy or wild and needs to gain some control.
6. Also point out when someone is going too slowly and can speed up.

4.1F Friendship Cards— Appropriate Body Behavior

Time: 10–15 minutes

Purpose: The friendship cards are used as a visual reminder for the children to reinforce the concept that has been taught.

Materials: Friendship Cards in Appendix A:

- My Personal Space
- What We Say if Someone Is in Our Personal Space

Preparation: See directions in "How to Use This Book" on page 12.

Procedure: See directions in "How to Use This Book" on page 12.

Lesson 4.2

Body Needs—Strengths and Weaknesses

Introduction/Overview

The goal of this lesson is to help the children develop an understanding of their body needs. We caution adults to be aware of whether they are using this to develop a "belief of inability." We want this lesson to be about achieving instead of limiting. That is why we want to develop the concept of needing help instead of weakness. We want the children to understand that need is not equal to deficiency. We also want the children to develop a need to achieve things on their own.

Teaching Concepts

- We can all do active things.
- We can all learn to do things on our own.
- Sometimes we need help.

Attitudinal Approach

- Many people do not really look at the needs they have when it comes to body awareness.

Lesson Objectives

- Children will identify their body abilities.
- Children will identify the activities they enjoy.
- Children will identify those activities with which they need help.
- Children will identify their friends' body abilities.
- Children will modify games to meet their friends' needs.

Lesson Introduction

Brainstorm for Key Concepts

Have children develop lists to refer to by asking specific questions. Use the directions found on page 11 in the "How to Use This Book" section. *Time:* 10–15 minutes.

- Things I do well
- Things with which I need help
- Places we get help

Activities

4.2A Body Strengths and Weaknesses Collage

Time: 15–20 minutes

Purpose: In this activity, the children make a visual representation of what they were just discussing. The intention is to help them create a positive attitude toward their own challenges.

Materials: Two large posters, crayons, markers, glue, construction paper, white drawing paper

Preparation: Label the top of one poster "Things We Do Well" and the other "Getting Help."

Procedure:

1. Have children draw one picture of themselves doing something that they do well and one of someone helping them with something that is a challenge.

2. Have each child cut out the picture and back it on construction paper and put it on the appropriate poster.

3. When poster is finished, revisit it and have children volunteer to share what they drew and explain how they feel when someone shares with them.

4.2B Spot Twister

Time: 10–15 minutes

Purpose: In this game, children will move their bodies in odd, contorted ways to reach the spots. It will give the children an opportunity to see how much they can and cannot do. It will also show the children the physical limitations of their friends. This is a great way to show that physical limitations do not mean a lack of fun.

Materials: Polyspots

Preparation: Lay out spots around the play area so they are within a reaching distance of one another and randomized.

Procedure:

1. Have each child start out on a spot.

2. Explain to them that you will call out colors and they will need to have at least three body parts touching different colors at all times.

3. Call out different colors for the children to have to touch with some body part.

4. Make it more challenging and name a body part and color that the children have to use.

4.2C Disability Obstacle Course

Time: 10–15 minutes

Purpose: In this activity, the children go through a simple obstacle course but will do it with a new physical challenge.

Materials: Scarves, gross motor equipment, tape, index cards

Preparation: Write a challenge on cards, one for each child (examples: can't see, only one leg, broken arm, can't talk).

Procedure:

1. Have children use the equipment to make an obstacle course for themselves.

2. After course is finished, have the children pick a challenge from the deck of cards.

3. Use the scarves and the tape and help the children to challenge themselves.

4. As a group or in pairs, have the children go through the obstacle course.

5. After going through, have the children take some time to discuss the experience and what they need to remember when picking games with friends.

4.2D Problem-Solving Game

Time: 15–20 minutes

Purpose: The purpose of this game is to have the children remake the games so that everyone can play and be involved.

Materials: A few games (board games, gross motor and art activities), poster board, and markers

Preparation: Pick the games that you know some of the children have difficulty with. Write the names of the games, one on each poster board.

Procedure:

1. Talk about what we have learned about the needs of our friends.

2. Have the children review their needs and what they have learned about making things accessible for everyone.

3. Show the games you have picked.

4. Go through each game and have the children share what they or a friend of theirs would have trouble with in each game. Suggest the children share information about friends they have at home or in their families.

5. After getting a list of three or four challenges for each game, go back and brainstorm with the children how we could change the game so that everyone can play (example: use memory picture cards instead of word cards for someone who cannot read).

6. Have the children then try to play the games in the new modified way.

7. Have children come back in a discussion group and talk about whether it is fun or if something new should be tried.

8. Finish by sharing that even the adaptive way of doing things can be fun.

4.2E Friendship Cards— Appropriate Body Behavior

Time: 10–15 minutes

Purpose: The friendship cards are used as a visual reminder for the children to reinforce the concept that has been taught.

Materials: Friendship Cards in Appendix A:

- Things I Do Well
- Things I Need Help With
- People Who Help Me

Preparation: See directions in "How to Use This Book" on page 12.

Procedure: See directions in "How to Use This Book" on page 12.

esson 4.3

Personal Play Space

Introduction/Overview

In this lesson, we are looking to help children understand that there exist bubbles around them and other people, which are defined as personal space. We want to give the children an understanding of this invisible space and have a sensory experience that will support this concept. Children with social challenges have difficulty noticing the nonverbal body language cues that are the key to social awareness. Because of this, little details are not noticed. These are base concepts for the topics that we explore in social awareness, self-image, and self-control. It would be beneficial to review these concepts.

Teaching Concepts

- Everyone has a different personal space bubble.
- Not everyone has the ability to perceive other people's personal space.

Attitudinal Approach

- Not everyone has the same body needs and sensitivities.
- Everyone has a different comfort level in sensory sensitivities.

Lesson Objectives

- Children will have a physical experience of their own personal space.
- Children will identify the appropriate personal physical space needed in relationships with various people.
- Children will learn and use strategies to regulate personal space.

Lesson Introduction

Brainstorm for Key Concepts

Have children develop lists to refer to by asking specific questions. Use the directions found on page 11 in the "How to Use This Book" section. *Time:* 10–15 minutes.

- What is personal space?
- When do we need to check personal space?
- Have you ever had someone come into your personal space? What happened? How did it feel?
- What do we say if someone is in our personal space?

Activities

4.3A Making Our Own Personal Space Circle

Time: 10–15 minutes

Purpose: This activity is designed to help children have a physical experience of what personal space is and what their comfort level is. The activity will add a visual aspect to the concept of personal space.

Materials: Poster board (one for every two children), various colored markers

Preparation: Draw an X in the center of each poster.

Procedure:

1. Have the children take turns standing on an X in the middle of the poster.

2. Have the children draw a circle around themselves that will be their personal space.

3. Have the rest of the class line up on the edge of the circle and ask the child if she or he feels comfortable or if she or he needs to have the group step back.

4. Have the child draw a new circle for the class to stand on.

5. Repeat the process with each child.

6. Compare the circles.

7. Save circles for activities in Lesson 4.4: Body Privacy.

4.3B Personal Space Freeze Dance

Time: 5–10 minutes

Purpose: In this activity, children experience how difficult it is to keep appropriate personal space when involved in an active game. It will give them the opportunity to check their personal space often while in an activity.

Materials: Masking tape or polyspots, music

Preparation: Put spots down on the ground in a random pattern using masking tape or a sit-upons like polyspots. Make sure some of the spots are close to each other and others are spaced well apart.

Procedure:

1. Have each child get on a spot, and have each child check to make sure that no one is in her or his personal space.

2. Instruct the children that they will play a freeze dance and that when the music stops they need to get on a spot.

3. Play music and stop after a short time.

4. Ask all the children to look and see if anyone is too close to them. If a child thinks someone is too close, have him or her move or have the child ask the person who is too close to move to another spot using sweet words.

4.3C Friendship Cards—
Appropriate Body Behavior

Time: 15–20 minutes

Purpose: The friendship cards are used as a visual reminder for the children to reinforce the concept that has been taught.

Materials: Friendship Cards in Appendix A:

- My Personal Space
- What We Say if Someone Is in Our Personal Space

Preparation: See directions in "How to Use This Book" on page 12.

Procedure: See directions in "How to Use This Book" on page 12.

Lesson 4.4

Body Privacy

Introduction/Overview

In this lesson, we discuss body privacy: both our own and that of our friends. We chose to separate this from personal play space in order to give it the attention it deserves. Many children, with disabilities and without, fall victim to inappropriate touching by adults and even other children. Many children with disabilities get labeled as physically aggressive simply because they have never been properly taught appropriate body behavior. We want to empower children by educating them as to what is safe and appropriate when interacting with others and what to do when things cross the line of appropriate behavior. In this and the next lesson, our intention is to avoid as much shame as possible in order to make sure the children do not develop poor body concepts. We discuss how to keep your own body private and how to respect others' body privacy. We also address safety and what it means and what to do when someone uses inappropriate touch.

Teaching Concepts

- Our body is our own and we keep it to ourselves.
- Our friends' bodies are private, and we respect that by using our hands appropriately.
- We tell Mom, Dad, and doctors when someone touches us and where.

Attitudinal Approach

- Our comfort with the subject makes a very big impact on how children will react to the information.
- We need to be comfortable discussing sensitive topics.
- This is a positive opportunity, and we should be excited to help our children be safe.

Lesson Objectives

- Children will identify the areas of the body that are private.
- Children will identify and use appropriate forms of touch with others.
- Children will identify what to do if their own body privacy is invaded.

Lesson Introduction

Concept Map—Body Privacy

Have children develop a concept map (see Figure 4.1) to refer to by asking leading questions. Use the directions found on page 11 in the "How to Use This Book" section. *Time:* 10–15 minutes.

Figure 4.1 Body Privacy Concept Map

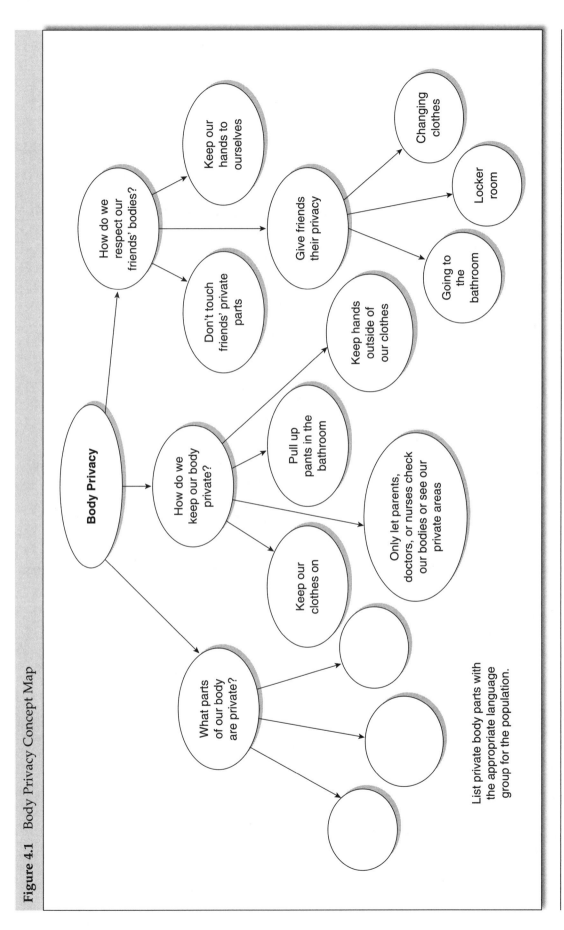

Activities

4.4A Appropriate Pyramids

Time: 15–20 minutes

Purpose: This is a visual exercise to help illustrate the "privacy level" for different parts of the body. We need to focus on the positive aspect of keeping our bodies private and safe.

Materials: Worksheet 4.1 Appropriate Pyramid on page 198 in Appendix B, markers, poster

Preparation: Make a copy of the pyramid for each child. Make a large poster of the pyramid.

Procedure:

1. Brainstorm a list of people in the children's lives.

2. Introduce the different categories of people in the Appropriate Pyramid and have the children give examples of the people they know in each category.

3. Write on poster the appropriate behaviors that children can do with these groups of people.

   a. Parents/doctor/grandparents—kiss, hug, sit on lap, help get dressed or undressed, check private areas, talk to

   b. Teacher/nurse—go to for help with body issues when sick, get help in the bathroom, put arm around, give high five, hold hand, talk to

   c. Aunts/uncles/cousins/brother/sister—hug, kiss on cheek, ask to get parent when needing help with body issue, help with clothes or bath when parent says it is okay, put arm around, give high five, hold hand, talk to

   d. School friends/family friends/close neighbors—put arm around, give high five, hold hand, wave to, say "Hi," go to in an emergency, talk to

   e. Community helpers/other neighbors—wave to, say "Hi," go to in an emergency, talk to

   f. Strangers—smile, say "Hi"

4. Have children fill in one or two answers on their own pyramids.

4.4B What's Missing?— Dress Up Game

Time: 15–20 minutes

Purpose: In this activity, children use dolls to practice appropriate dress.

Materials: Any baby doll or stuffed animal that can fit into doll clothes. Children can be asked to bring a doll from home with clothes.

Preparation: Make bags of outfits with one item missing; make a basket with the missing items. Dress each doll inappropriately, both by putting clothes on wrong and forgetting to cover private body parts.

Procedure:

1. Split children into groups and give each team a doll.

2. Have the groups share what they observe to be wrong with the way the dolls are dressed.

3. Hand out bags of clothes and ask children to redress dolls appropriately.

 ## 4.4C Question Scavenger Hunt

Time: 5–10 minutes

Purpose: This activity is a fun way to test how well the children retained the information in the concept map. It is a combination of quiz game and scavenger hunt.

Materials: Two large posters with an outline of a body, clothing cut out to fit the bodies on the poster (use Worksheets 4.2 Paper Doll (page 199) and 4.3 Paper Doll Clothes (page 200) in Appendix B as guides), index cards, and questions based on the concept map

Preparation:

1. Make the posters and clothes.

2. Write questions based on the answers the group came up with for the concept map on the index cards.

3. Hide the clothes for the poster around the room.

Procedure:

1. Split the class into two groups.

2. When it is the group's turn, have one child pick a card and read the card to the group.

3. Children raise their hands to answer the questions.

4. When the children get the answer right, give them a clue to where an item of clothing is hidden in the room. When they find it, they can put the clothes on the body for their team.

5. The team that dresses its body poster first wins.

4.4D Make a Book or PSA Poster

Time: 15–20 minutes

Purpose: In this activity, we work out an easy-to-follow process for children to use to get help if their body space is invaded.

Materials: Posters, art materials

Preparation:

1. Have children discuss what it means when someone invades their body privacy and what they need to do if that happens. Use leading questions to help them come to steps that are similar to the following:

   a. Tell them, "Don't touch me."

   b. Call for help.

   c. Tell an adult what happened.

2. Have children make a list of things they would say to other kids to let them know that people should not invade their body privacy.

Procedure:

1. Split the children into groups of two or three.

2. Have each group make a poster to hang in the halls that will help their friends to know what to do if someone invades their body privacy.

4.4E Friendship Cards—Appropriate Body Behavior

Time: 15–20 minutes

Purpose: The friendship cards are used as a visual reminder for the children to reinforce the concept that has been taught.

Materials: Friendship Cards in Appendix A:

- Things We Do to Respect Our Friends' Body Privacy
- What I Do if Someone Invades My Body Privacy

Preparation: See directions in "How to Use This Book" on page 12.

Procedure: See directions in "How to Use This Book" on page 12.

Generalization and Consistency

- When children accidentally touch someone inappropriately, refer them to the friendship cards of appropriate touch.
- Treat as an opportunity for teaching and avoid judgmental attitudes.

Lesson 4.5

Modesty/Hygiene

Introduction/Overview

We define "modesty" as the appropriate way we outwardly portray our bodies in the way we dress. We have paired modesty with hygiene in this chapter to help children develop an outward image that attracts others to them. We live in a very visual society, and the way someone looks affects others' impression. Many children who have difficulty with social interaction do not have a firm grasp on proper hygiene and dress. In this lesson, we look at modesty and hygiene and how we dress and take care of our bodies.

Teaching Concepts

- Keeping ourselves clean and healthy helps us to be happy and have fun.
- Staying clean and healthy helps us to keep and make friends.
- Keeping our bodies clean, healthy, and dressed makes it easier for others to be our friend.

Attitudinal Approach

- Accept that children have trouble grasping certain safety concepts.
- We are avoiding shame. We can be private about our bodies without feeling ashamed of them.

Lesson Objectives

- Children will identify what habits are needed in the day to keep proper hygiene.
- Children will identify why proper hygiene is important for their health.
- Children will list why proper hygiene helps them to make and keep friends.

Lesson Introduction

Brainstorm for Key Concepts

Have children develop lists to refer to by asking specific questions. Use the directions found on page 11 in the "How to Use This Book" section. *Time:* 10–15 minutes

- What do we do in the morning to be neat and clean?
- What do we do during the day to be neat and clean?
- What do we do at night to be neat and clean?
- How does keeping neat and clean help us to have and keep friends?

Activities

4.5A Washing of the Germs Game

Time: 5–10 minutes

Purpose: Children get a real sense of how difficult it is to keep their hands clean and how hard they need to wash.

Materials: Glitter (green and purple are best), water, soap, sinks/water tubs, paper towels, drop cloth, a hand-washing chart using pictures and words

Preparation: Make sure there are enough paper towels for all children; lay drop cloths over the area where the activity will be done.

Procedure:

1. Review the concept development that was done in the beginning about how it is important to keep clean.

2. Show the glitter to the children and let them know that you are pretending that they are the germs for the day.

3. Using the hand-washing chart to practice the proper way to wash hands.

4. Have each child come and put her or his hand in the "germ" mix and get germs on her or his hands. Then have the children use the water in the tubs to wash off the glitter germs.

5. Point out how hard they need to work to get their hands clean.

4.5B Dress the Best Game

Time: 10–15 minutes

Purpose: The purpose of this game is to have the children look at the different ways people can get dressed in a fun and silly way. It gives children the opportunity to look critically at someone's attire without attacking anyone's self-esteem.

Materials: Worksheet 4.2 Paper Doll on page 199 in Appendix B

Preparation: Make copies of the paper doll.

Procedure:

1. Split the children into groups of two to four.

2. Have the children color in the paper dolls. Have half the children color in well-dressed dolls based on the brainstorming and half color in messy kids.

3. After the pictures are colored, have the children cut the people into threes and put the threes into piles according to top, bottom, and middle. Shuffle each pile.

4. Each child is to pick piece from each pile and put the person puzzle together. The children need to say which part of the body is best-dressed and tell what should change about the other parts.

5. Have each child take a turn.

6. For small groups or one-to-ones, make a best-dressed flip book and make funny people and discuss the parts that are best-dressed and what should be changed.

4.5C Make a Book to Teach Others About a Topic

Time: 30–40 minutes

(This activity may require two separate class times to complete.)

Purpose: This activity brings together the concepts in this lesson.

Materials: Paper, markers

Preparation: Review the posters and brainstorm concepts the children have created so far.

Procedure:

1. Have the children make a book about privacy using construction paper.

2. Tell children that they are making a book to teach others what they have learned.

3. Refer to the brainstorming materials from lesson introductions to help children decide what they want to add to their book.

4. Share the books and make a display.

4.5D Friendship Cards— Appropriate Body Behavior

Time: 15–20 minutes

Purpose: The friendship cards are used as a visual reminder for the children to reinforce the concept that has been taught.

Materials: Friendship Cards in Appendix A:

- What We Do in the Morning to be Neat and Clean
- What We Do During the Day to be Neat and Clean
- What We Do at Night to Be Neat and Clean

Preparation: See directions in "How to Use This Book" on page 12.

Procedure: See directions in "How to Use This Book" on page 12.

Generalization and Consistency

- Hang PSA posters.
- Use a daily chart and give out stars for cleanliness to children, with prizes at the end of the week.
- Have children self-evaluate hygiene and modesty by giving themselves 3 to 5 stars on a list of 8 to 10 items of the things they do the best and 1 to 2 checks on things they would like to improve. Revisit the chart in 2 to 3 weeks.

Lesson 4.6

Appropriate Bodies in Different Environments

Introduction/Overview

In this lesson, we help children identify when and why we use different speeds in different places. Many children have not been taught how to observe an environment and assess the way their body speed affects their social interactions. The goal is to show each child that there are appropriate times and places for different speeds and how to know what to do.

Teaching Concepts

- Everyone has different sensory needs.
- All body speeds are good (even fast body).
- We can control our body speeds with movement, touch, sight, and smell.
- There is an appropriate body speed for every situation.

Attitudinal Approach

- Everyone has different sensory solutions.
- We need to give people the time they need for their own sensory input.

Lesson Objectives

- Children will identify what their body speed is at different times during the day.
- Children will accept sensory suggestion to help change their body speed.
- Children will identify the different body speeds.
- Children will identify what their body speed is at different times during the day.

Lesson Introduction

Brainstorm for Key Concepts

Have children develop lists to refer to by asking specific questions. Use the directions found on page 11 in the "How to Use This Book" section. *Time:* 10–15 minutes.

- Using place cards, have children make a brainstorming list of how they should act in the different environments. Put them in categories of fast, focused, or slow. Then ask the children to list answers to the following questions:
  o What helps us to slow down?
  o What helps us to speed up?
  o Why should we try to change the speed our body is going?

Activities

4.6A Pictures of Each Body Speed   *Time:* 15–20 minutes

Purpose: This activity helps children review the different body speeds and gives them the opportunity to act out each level.

Materials: Polaroid camera, film to take two to three pictures of each child, glue

Preparation: None

Procedure:

1. Either during or after the Freeze Dance activity, take pictures of the children moving and acting out each level.

2. Have each child tell you which level he or she was acting out in each picture.

4.6B Brainstorm Words to Match Speeds   *Time:* 5–10 minutes

Purpose: The purpose of this activity is to help children create a greater understanding of body speeds and their meaning. This activity is good for visual learners who enjoy reading and words.

Materials: Lists of locations and how we act from the lesson introduction (a new one or one that has already been created), paper, and markers

Preparation: None

Procedure:

1. Have the children brainstorm different words that can represent the body speeds.
   a. Colors (fast = red, orange)
   b. Physical sensations (fast = tight, prickly)
   c. Temperatures (fast = hot)
   d. Activities that you would do (slow = sleep, listen to quiet music)
   e. Adjectives (fast = wild, excited)

2. Have each child pick a word, write it in bubble letters, and decorate it.

4.6C Matching Game of Pictures to Speed

Time: 15–20 minutes

Purpose: This activity reinforces the concepts and gives children the opportunity to observe the concepts in others.

Materials: Place cards, Polaroid pictures of the different body speeds

Preparation: None

Procedure:

1. Make two piles: one of the photos of the children and one of the location cards.

2. Have the children in teams go through and match the pictures with the location that is appropriate.

3. Have children discuss the different locations and why they matched the pictures that they did.

4.6D Musical Hoops

Time: 5–10 minutes

Purpose: This activity gives children propreoceptic input through jumping, as well as vestibular input through running and moving around the hoop.

Materials: A hoop for each child, music

Preparation: None

Procedure:

1. Have the children pick a hoop and find a place in the room to put their hoop down.

2. Move children around if they are too close to one another, making sure those children who need more room have enough.

3. When the music starts, have the children do a particular movement.

4. When the music stops, the children freeze.

5. Have the children do a movement for three to four freezes, and then suggest a new movement. Suggested movements: Jump in and out of the hoop, run around the outside of the hoop, run around the inside of the hoop, walk around the hoop with one foot on the inside and one on the outside.

4.6E Don't Break the Ice
by Milton Bradley

Time: 15–20 minutes

Purpose: This is a great game to help children who have trouble controlling their impulses. To be successful in the game, you need to control the rate and strength of tapping. This is a challenge for some children, and this is a fun way to help them to work on it.

Materials: The game

Preparation: See game directions.

Procedure:

1. Have a discussion with the children about how the game is played and how they need to use gentle banging.

2. Set up the game as described in the directions and allow the children to bang the ice cubes as hard as they want for a test and to let them get it out of their system.

3. Play the game as explained in the directions.

4.6F Pete's a Pizza

Time: 15–20 minutes

Purpose: In this activity, the children will see a child doing sensory input games with his family.

Materials: Pete's a Pizza by William Steig, paper plates, construction paper, and crayons

Preparation: Cut out red circles for pepperoni. Cut construction paper into small pieces to be cheese or use leftovers from paper shredder.

Procedure:

1. Read the book *Pete's a Pizza* by William Steig aloud to the children.

2. Have the children guess how Pete's body felt before his father made him into a pizza.

3. Have the children guess how Pete felt after his dad made him into a pizza.

4. Have a sensory experience with the children by acting out the book. Have adults go from child to child to turn the children into pizzas or have children pair off and turn each other into pizzas.

5. Do an art project where children make pizzas out of paper plates. Have children color and cut out the pizza toppings, use markers to color the paper plate with "pizza sauce," and glue the topping on.

6. Another option is to allow the children to make pizzas out of playdough.

4.6G Freeze Dance With Various Music Speeds

Time: 5–10 minutes

Purpose: Through the use of music, this activity helps children experience and differentiate between various activities and body speeds.

Materials: Music with different speeds (suggestion: have examples of rock music, classical or lullaby music, and children's music at medium speed)

Preparation: None

Procedure:

1. Have children find a place in the room.

2. Tell the children that you want them to guess which body speed they should use to move and dance to the music. Tell them that when the music stops they should freeze.

3. Play a piece of music and have the children yell out the body speed they think it is. It will be difficult for children to guess "focused" and "fast." Play the examples repeatedly to help them become accustomed to each.

4. Have the children dance to the beat of the music and demonstrate the different levels of movement. Help the children to understand slowing down for low body speed music, speeding up for the fast body speed music, and finding the balance between the two for focused body speed music.

4.6H Musical Islands

Time: 10–15 minutes

Purpose: Musical islands is played like musical chairs, but children are asked to share spots as some spots are taken away. The object of the game is to have all the children sharing one spot at the end without anyone getting knocked down. This game helps children go from moving at a fast pace to moving carefully so that no one gets knocked over. This activity can be used with many of the lessons, and we use this as sensory filler in our session just to give the children move-around time.

Materials: Polyspots or construction paper taped to the ground, music, and player

Preparation: Lay spots out on the ground spaced one to two feet apart.

Procedure:

1. Have children find a spot of their own to stand on.

2. When the music starts, have the children get off the spots and dance around the room.

3. When the music stops, the children each pick a new spot to stand on.

4. After two or three stops in the music, start by taking one or two spots away from the children when the music stops.

5. The children need to share spots. Even having one toe on the spot counts.

4.6I Silly Speed Pictures
Time: 10–15 minutes

Purpose: We use this activity to help the children to begin brainstorming the different things that they should use their body speeds for.

Materials: Paper and art supplies, poster, place cards

Preparation: None

Procedure:

1. Brainstorm what is good to do when you are at the different speeds.

2. Draw pictures of activities/experiences for each level of body speed.

3. Have children tale turns picking cards from a pile. Have children identify what speed is needed in the place they chose.

4. Have children guess what would happen if they use the wrong speed in the environments (example: using a fast speed in a library). Draw pictures of the different silly speeds.

4.6J Friendship Cards— Appropriate Body Behavior
Time: 10–15 minutes

Purpose: The friendship cards are used as a visual reminder for the children to reinforce the concept that has been taught.

Materials: Friendship Cards in Appendix A:

- How We Slow Our Body When It Is Too Fast
- How We Get Our Body Moving When It Is Too Slow
- Places for Fast Body Speed
- Places for Slow Body Speed
- Places for Focused Body

Preparation: See directions in "How to Use This Book" on page 12.

Procedure: See directions in "How to Use This Book" on page 12.

Generalization and Consistency

- Refer children to friendship cards for suggestions for changing body speeds.
- Offer sensory input to children before and after times of focus to help the children attend to what is going on.

UNIT 5

Appropriate Emotional Behavior

Emotional education is very important for children at as early an age as possible. Children's emotions develop through their experiences, and they need the best tools they can get their hands on to express and deal with the emotions they feel. In the past, we have taken a very careful approach to emotional education. We have observed two factors in emotional education that can have a negative affect on children's development: (1) the attitude that is conveyed about emotions and (2) the strategies they are taught to employ. When developing emotional awareness and vocabulary, there are a lot of terms that children need to be introduced to. Over the years we have looked at many of the resources that introduce emotional language to children, and one thing we have found is that a majority of resources are very heavy on teaching negative emotions. If you choose an emotion game and count how many negative words are introduced and how many positive words are represented, you will find that in most cases, there are many more negative vocabulary words introduced to children. All children need a working emotional vocabulary to express the entire rang of emotions, not just the negative ones. In this unit, we focus on developing a well-rounded emotional vocabulary, strengthening children's ability to identify emotions in others, and expressing their own emotions in useful ways.

SOCIAL GOALS

- Child will be able to identify and describe a wide variety of emotions when observing them in others in a variety of environments.

- Child will be able to identify her or his own emotions when asked, both when having the emotion and when recalling an experience.
- Child will be able to identify the appropriate emotional response to different social situations when given the situation.
- Child will be able to identify a peer's emotion or feeling by looking at his or her facial expression or by asking how he or she is feeling.
- After a conflict with a peer, the child will be able to label her or his own emotion before, during, and after the conflict.

Lesson 5.1

What Are Emotions and How Do We Show Them?

Introduction/Overview

All students need a working vocabulary and understanding of emotions in order to use them in different social settings. Behavioral responses do not always give us the best clue to what a child is feeling. Some children express fear with aggression and some with tears. Without a working ability to communicate what they are feeling, children can be misunderstood and become frustrated.

Teaching Concepts

- We can say the emotion we are feeling to help ourselves and others to know what we are feeling.
- We want to learn more emotion words to label and explain our emotions more clearly.

Attitudinal Approach

- Certain activities in this lesson, if not performed with care, can damage children's self-image, so we must always choose our words carefully.

Lesson Objective

- Children will be introduced to the concept of appropriate emotional behavior.

Lesson Introduction

Brainstorm for Key Concepts

Have children develop lists to refer to by asking specific questions. Use the directions found on page 11 in the "How to Use This Book" section. *Time: 10–15 minutes.*

- Have children brainstorm a list of 10 positive emotion words they know.
- Have children brainstorm a list of 10 negative behaviors.
- Have a children think of a time when they have felt each of these emotions.

Activities

5.1A Emotion Match Game

Time: 5–10 minutes

Purpose: Children associate facial expressions with appropriate emotions.

Materials: Cards with the 20 emotion words from the brainstorming list, Emotion Flashcards on page 206 in Appendix B with facial expressions corresponding to words brainstormed

Preparation: Copy emotion words onto index cards. Glue corresponding facial expressions on index cards.

Procedure:

1. Lay out emotion cards faceup and have children find the cards that correspond. Take turns picking the cards and saying what the emotion is. This may be difficult for the children at first. This might need to be played more than once for children to get it.

2. Then play the game with the face cards turned up and the emotion words facedown in a pile. In this version, the child has to find the face that matches the card.

3. Finally, play as a memory game with all cards facedown where children will try to find the matches. Not all groups will be ready for this level of play developmentally.

5.1B Emotion Snack

Time: 10–15 minutes

Purpose: This is an artistic way for children to express their emotions and practice reading others' feelings.

Materials: Paper plates, a variety of appropriate snack foods in different shapes such as pretzels, camera for pictures. Make sure to be aware of the food allergies of the children you are working with.

Preparation: Cut food into appropriate bite sizes for the snack. Place in bowls.

Procedure:

1. Give each child a plate and have the children use the food to make different faces. When they are done, instruct them to show you and take a picture of each.

2. Encourage the children to share what emotion they have made. Have children make more than one plate if there is time.

3. For a greater challenge, print out each picture of food faces. Display the pictures. Have children guess the emotions their friends have created. Point out that sometimes it is difficult to figure out people's emotions from their faces.

5.1C Emotion Charades

Time: 5–20 minutes depending on number of children

Purpose: This game helps children role-play their emotions and practice identifying the emotions they observe in others. It is also a great way to illustrate how difficult emotions can be to read in some people.

Materials: Index cards with emotion words

Preparation: None

Procedure:

1. Have children take turns picking an emotion from the emotion words and acting out an emotion.

2. Have other children guess the emotion they are portraying. If children are having a difficult time guessing, prompt them to ask their friends, "How do you feel?" Point out that sometimes we cannot guess what someone is feeling and need to ask.

3. In some cases, children who are acting out emotions will overdramatize the emotion. Give the child feedback about whether what she or he was acting out really portrays the emotion. Let other children give their version of the emotion and compare.

5.1D Friendship Cards— Appropriate Emotional Behavior

Time: 5–10 minutes

Purpose: The friendship cards are used as a visual reminder for the children to reinforce the concept that has been taught.

Materials: Friendship Card in Appendix A: Emotions I Know

Preparation: See directions in "How to Use This Book" on page 12.

Procedure: See directions in "How to Use This Book" on page 12.

Note: Create a personal emotional dictionary with the children. Make multiple copies of the "Emotions I Know" card and have the children create one for each of the brainstormed emotions. Add to it at later times when a child has experienced a complex emotion and needs to have it defined.

Generalization and Consistency

- In books and other curriculum materials, look for opportunities to point out individuals emotions and have children identify them.
- Add to brainstorming list when a new emotion is discussed to help children expand their emotional vocabulary.

Lesson 5.2

Choosing How We React

Introduction/Overview

In this lesson, we focus on the different reactions that a child can use in different situations. The goal is to help children see that different emotions will get you different results in social situations.

Teaching Concepts

- There is a range of intensity in the way we can react, and it should match the seriousness of the situation.
- We can control how we react, and that will help us to get what we want.

Attitudinal Approach

- Certain activities in this lesson, if not performed with care, can damage the children's self-image, so we must always choose our words carefully.

Lesson Objectives

- Child will identify an appropriate emotional response to different social and conflict situations.
- Child will be able to predict different outcomes from different emotional responses in the same social situation.

Lesson Introduction

Brainstorm for Key Concepts

Have children develop lists to refer to by asking specific questions. Use the directions found on page 11 in the "How to Use This Book" section. *Time:* 5–10 minutes.

- Using the emotion words, choose two or three negative and positive words. For younger children, choose simple emotions, and for older children, challenge them with more vague words.
- Have children brainstorm more situations where they have felt these emotions and list them.
- Point out how emotions can be found in many different places.

Activities

5.2A Rate the Situation

Time: 10–15 minutes

Purpose: Illustrate that there are different levels of intensity of reaction to situations, and each of the reactions we choose will get us a different result.

Materials: Large white paper, pictures of different emotions based on the brainstorming

Preparation:

1. Choose one of the positive and one of the negative emotions.

2. Create a vertical chart on a poster board with the emotion listed on the top.

Procedure:

1. Have the children act out an extreme version of the emotion. Use a picture to depict the emotion in its extreme. Then have children act out the emotion in a subdued way. (Example: "Everyone show me your maddest face. Now show me what it looks like when you are just a little bit mad.")

2. Put the extreme face on the top of the chart and the subdued face at the bottom.

3. As a class or in a small group, have the children rate each of the situations they added to the brainstorming list. Have them discuss how intensely they should react to each situation and put it on the chart.

4. Review the different choices in a group and give children feedback on their choices.

5.2B Emotion Meter

Time: 15–20 minutes

Purpose: The goal of this activity is to help children to see the extremes of different emotions and begin to gauge what an appropriate response would be in different situations.

Materials: Letter-size piece of poster board or oak tag per child, small 2-inch square of construction paper, string, tape, Worksheet 5.1 My Emotion Meter on page 201 in Appendix B

Preparation: Cut string about 25 inches long (twice the length of a piece of paper), copy the Emotion Meter for each child, punch a hole in the top and bottom of poster board near where the arrow in the "meter" will be.

Procedure:

1. These can be created in many ways depending on the level of the children and the particular needs of the group.

    a. Choose an emotion and instruct the children to draw the different levels of that one emotion from extreme at the top to mild at the bottom (example: for happy, the top circle would have some wildly ecstatic face, and the bottom would have a face that is mildly smiling).

    b. Instruct children to draw faces that range from positive at the top to negative at the bottom.

    c. Choose pictures of emotion in a particular range that the children need to understand and have them cut and paste them in order from top to bottom. Base this choice on the emotion that the group is having challenges with.

2. Have the children draw a picture of themselves on the construction paper.

3. Glue the meter on the front of the poster board.

4. Thread the string through the holes in the poster board and tie in the back.

5. Tape the child's picture of himself or herself on the string so it can move up and down the meter.

6. Ask questions of the children about how they would feel in different situations. Have them move the picture of themselves up and down to see where they would go. Have them hold the meters up and share their choices. Give feedback about the appropriateness of their choices and discuss with the group the outcome of their choices.

5.2C Friendship Cards—Appropriate Emotional Behavior

Time: 5–10 minutes

Purpose: The friendship cards are used as a visual reminder for the children to reinforce the concept that has been taught.

Materials: Friendship Card in Appendix A: Emotions I Know

Preparation: See directions in "How to Use This Book" on page 12.

Procedure: See directions in "How to Use This Book" on page 12.

Generalization and Consistency

- When different issues come up in the classroom, use them as an opportunity to add to the situation chart and continue the discussion on the intensity of different issues.
- Use emotion meters to help children to express how they feel in different situation. Allow the children to use the visual meter to help them express themselves when they are they are overwhelmed and may be having difficulty verbally sharing how they feel.

Lesson 5.3

Staying Calm When We Don't Get Along

Introduction/Overview

In this lesson, children are introduced to different techniques that can be used to help them calm down. The goal is to help children to see how these exercises help them solve their problems and feel better overall. The key for success in this lesson definitely lies in how much these techniques are communicated to others in the child's life. Parents, family members, teachers, and therapists need to be consistent with supporting the child in his or her attempts to stay calm and in reminding the child what these strategies are.

Teaching Concepts

- The best way to work out the conflicts we have is by staying calm and communicating our wants to others.
- There is a solution to every situation.
- It is easier for people to understand what we want and help us when we are calm.

Attitudinal Approach

- Everyone gets upset and has a right to his or her emotions.
- Everyone has the ability to control her or his emotions and to express them in a useful way.

Lesson Objectives

- Child will identify techniques and exercises that will help him or her calm down when overwhelmed.
- Child will use the techniques taught here to calm down in conflict situations.
- Child will request help in calming down from an adult when overwhelmed.

Lesson Introduction

Concept Map—Ways to Stay Calm

Have the children help develop a concept map (see Figure 5.1) by asking leading questions. Use the directions found on page 11 in the "How to Use This Book" section. *Time:* 10–15 minutes.

Figure 5.1 Ways to Stay Calm Concept Map

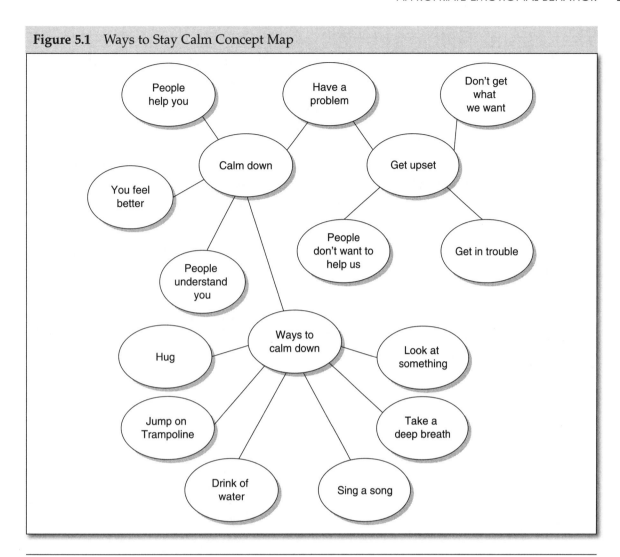

Activities

5.3A Bag of Calm

Time: 10–20 minutes

Purpose: Create a visual list of different items and activities that will help children calm down when they are overwhelmed.

Materials: Large posterboard, collage materials/magazines (pull out specific pages that show things that would be appropriate for the lesson)

Preparation: Draw a large bag on the poster board and label it "Bag of Calm."

Procedure:

1. Have children find pictures in magazines of the different things that help them to calm down.

2. Suggest things for children that are good calming items.

3. Cut and paste into the bag of calm. Hang in the room.

4. When children are beginning to get upset, refer them to the bag of calm and have them pick something that will help them calm down.

5.3B Feeling Masks

Time: 10–15 minutes

Purpose: To practice identifying emotions in peers and develop the perceptive skills to understand a peer's point of view

Materials: Paper plates, art materials, popsicle sticks

Preparation: None

Procedure:

1. Have children use art materials and make faces of different emotions from the emotion chart. Either have each child pick the emotion he or she wants to portray or assign emotions randomly.

2. Glue the popsicle sticks on the back for a mask.

3. Have children share their mask with the class. Ask each child to tell what she or he knows about the emotion. Use leading questions such as "What do you sound like when you are feeling this emotion?" "Where do you feel this emotion?" or "What will make you feel this?"

5.3C Excited/Calm— Red Light Green Light

Time: 5–10 minutes

Purpose: To have the children moving their bodies in both excited and calm movements to work on developing the ability to calm themselves

Materials: Two paper plates and two craft sticks

Preparation: On one plate, write the word *stop* in red on one side and the word *excited* in green on the other. On the other plate, write the word *stop* in red on one side and the word *calm* in green on the other. For nonreaders, use pictures that illustrate the two emotions.

Procedure:

1. Have the children line up on one side of an area where running would be safe. Explain to the children that they need to move wild and excited with the excited sign and slow and calm with the calm sign.

2. Hold both signs on red for the children to see. Turn the different signs to green to have the children move forward.

5.3D Friendship Cards—Appropriate Emotional Behavior

Time: 10–20 minutes

Purpose: The friendship cards are used as a visual reminder for the children to reinforce the concept that has been taught.

Materials: Friendship Card in Appendix A: Ways to Stay Calm

Preparation: See directions in "How to Use This Book" on page 12.

Procedure: See directions in "How to Use This Book" on page 12.

Generalization and Consistency

- Throughout the day, take time to regulate children and give them feedback about staying calm and focused.
- In conflict situations between peers, make sure to take the time to remind children to calm down so that they can solve the problem.
- Refer children to the concept map created in the lesson introduction to help them to remember the ways we can help ourselves to stay calm when we are in conflict.

Lesson 5.4

Appropriate Ways of Sharing Our Emotions

Introduction/Overview

In this lesson, we explore emotional expression. The importance of this lesson lies in finding the balance between emotional expression and emotional control. Our goal is to teach children that they have the right to their emotions and need to express them, but that at the same time, emotional control will help us to communicate what we want and solve our problems.

Teaching Concepts

- We all have a right to our emotions and a right to let people know how we feel.
- People do not always know what we are feeling, and we need to let them know in a safe way that they understand.
- People want to know what we feel and help us if we need it.

Attitudinal Approach

- Everyone needs to express her or his emotions, and we need to be accepting of that.
- We cannot always know how a child feels just by observing his or her behavior. It is our job to be detectives to understand children's needs until they develop the ability to share them.

Lesson Objective

- Child will use appropriate phrases to express emotions to peers.

Lesson Introduction

Brainstorm for Key Concepts

Have children develop lists to refer to by asking specific questions. Use the directions found on page 11 in the "How to use this book" section. *Time:* 10–20 minutes.

Emotion Sentences

- Take out the brainstorming list for the earlier parts of the unit. Review the information that you have developed with the children in the unit. Look at the list to find where children have shared situations in which they felt a particular emotion.
- Explain to children that in such situations we need to tell people what we feel so they can know and help us if we need it. Introduce the phrase "I feel _____ because _____."
- Go through the situations and have the children practice the emotion sentences. For the older children, use the phrase "I feel _____ because _____, so I want/need _____.

Activities

5.4A Emotion Bingo

Time: 15–20 minutes

Purpose: The children are given the opportunity to look at someone's face to interpret his or her feelings.

Materials: Emotion Bingo cards (page 202) and Emotion Flashcards (page 206) in Appendix B, bingo chips

Preparation: Make the emotion cards and bingo chips.

Procedure:

1. Each child picks a game card and enough chips for the card. Go over the rules for basic bingo and tell children that they need to fill the whole card in order to win.

2. The facilitator picks an emotion card from the pile and reads it to the children.

3. Then, the facilitator uses facial expressions to describe the emotion on the card. Give the children the opportunity to guess the emotion and then model the appropriate way of expressing emotions using phrases such as "I am feeling _____ because _____."

4. The children must locate that emotion on their game card and place a chip on the card.

5. Continue to play until some one gets bingo.

6. For younger children, overemphasize the emotion in your expression and use the more simplistic emotion cards. For older children, use a more subtle expression and include the more challenging emotion cards.

 ## 5.4B Friendship Scrapbook   *Time:* 15–20 minutes

Purpose: This is a good way to end the unit and to assess that the children have retained the different concepts.

Materials: Four to eight pieces of construction paper per child

Preparation: Gather all of the materials the children have used and created throughout the unit. Make extra copies of the pictures and visual aids.

Procedure:

1. Have children create a scrapbook of what they learned.

2. Prompt them to add what they learned, what they did, and what they think about emotions. You can have them make a page or two per lesson.

3. Have children share their books with each other.

5.4C Friendship Cards—Appropriate Emotional Behavior

Time: 5–10 minutes

Purpose: The friendship cards are used as a visual reminder for the children to reinforce the concept that has been taught.

Materials: Friendship Card in Appendix A: How to Share My Emotions

Preparation: See directions in "How to Use This Book" on page 12.

Procedure: See directions in "How to Use This Book" on page 12.

Generalization and Consistency

- Consistently prompt children with the appropriate ways to express their emotions in different environments.
- Have children share what they want to in the situation and turn emotion into a problem-solving opportunity.
- Give behavior-specific feedback when children share their emotions to reinforce the desired behaviors and to highlight what they are doing that will help them to solve their issues.

Appropriate Behavior in a Group

The skills that support positive abilities to work in a group include incorporating the concepts taught in the previous lessons. Those basic concepts give the children the foundation to interact in a group in a variety of environments. This unit was developed to take those previously learned skills and continue to generalize them into a group setting. This unit will not only deal with the skills necessary to work in a group but also allow each child the opportunity to use the strategies learned while interacting in a variety of activities.

SOCIAL GOALS

- Child will stay on topic when contributing to a group discussion in a classroom setting.
- Child will use positive language to share ideas and make suggestions on group projects.
- Child will use skills such as organizing others, giving directions, listening to ideas, and encouraging participation to interact in a group.
- Child will choose (unprompted/unfacilitated) to complete a game with a group.
- Child will respect personal space of peers and adults during a group activity.
- Child will use the skills taught to maintain focus and attention in a group environment.
- Child will use appropriate levels of movement and energy for different activities and environments.
- Child will use visual supports to increase participation and contributions to a group project.

Lesson 6.1

Listening in a Group

Introduction/Overview

This lesson develops the skills necessary to maintain interaction and communication in a group environment or with a leader of a group. The listening skills learned in Unit 2: Using Appropriate Eye Contact for Interaction, although they may have been taught in a group setting, focused on the eye contact skills needed for listening during one-to-one interactions. This lesson develops the listening skills necessary to maintain interaction in a group environment or with the leader of a group. Teaching strategies for listening increases the children's ability to focus and attend in group settings. Listening in a group setting only increases the challenge of attending for children who have auditory sensitivities. The extra noise, visual activity, and possible larger space add to the challenge of listening to retain information or show others you are listening. Once again, eye contact is both the cue to others you are listening and critical in assisting children's ability to attend.

Teaching Concepts

- Listening to the leader of the group helps you to follow along with the group.
- Listening to the other members of the group helps you to be a part of the group.
- Listening is the best way to show everyone in the group that you are involved in the activity.
- Looking at others helps you listen.

Attitudinal Approach

- Children with attentional and/or focusing challenges have an even harder time listening in a group.
- Some children may need additional visual supports (lists of directions) to help them follow in a group activity.
- The louder the environment, the harder it is to listen.

Lesson Objectives

- Children will increase their ability to participate in a group by learning how to listen in a group.
- Children will learn to ask for help when needed when they are not able to listen or attend.
- Children will learn how to listen to others' ideas and show respect for the idea even though they may not agree.
- Children will develop the ability to listen to others so they know when to contribute to a conversation.

Lesson Introduction

Concept Map—Listening in a Group

Have the children help develop a concept map (see Figure 6.1) by asking leading questions. Use the directions found on page 11 in the "How to Use This Book" section. *Time:* 5–15 minutes

- When teaching the concepts on the map provided, act out the wrong way of each aspect first to add humor to the children's learning. Then ask the children to help model the right way to listen and look interested.

Figure 6.1 Listening in a Group Concept Map

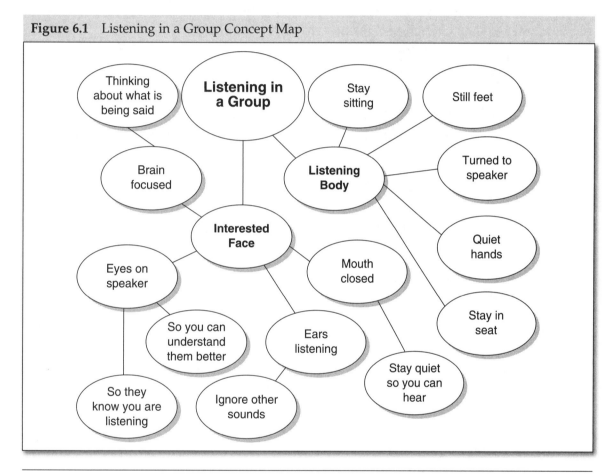

Activities

6.1A Gross Motor Group Cooperative— Parachute Keep Up, Skis, Tug-of-War *Time:* 10–15 minutes

Purpose: To help the children learn they need to listen to others to be able to participate. The Stride-R Ski by Sportime is perfect for pairs of children working together as a team. This is a great opportunity for children to learn listening skills. If you choose another gross motor cooperative activity, just adapt the directions to fit the activity. The intention behind the activity should remain the same.

Materials: Skis, parachute, rope

Preparation: Draw or use tape to make a start and a finish line.

Procedure:

1. Demonstrate how to use the skis.

2. Have children choose who will be in front and who will be in back (you may want to refer to the "Going First" section in the Games Unit).

3. Run the race.

4. Talk about what helped and what did not when racing.

5. Were they able to listen? Why?

6. Run the race again, reminding the children what they suggested that helped them in the race and what did not.

 ## 6.1B Noisy Whisper Down the Lane   *Time:* 5–15 minutes

Purpose: Improve listening skills for better attention in a group by providing the additional challenge of background noise.

Materials: None

Preparation: Make a list of directions that will be used in a group project. Gauge the complexity of the directions based on the age and skill level of the group.

Procedure:

1. Have children sit on the floor or in chairs next to each other in rows of four or five.

2. Explain the rules to Noisy Whisper Down the Lane.

3. Start each row by giving them the first directions.

4. Either have the last child write the direction down or tell it to an adult for the adult to write for the child.

5. When the direction is written, start again with the second direction until all the directions are given.

6. Have each row read their list and see how close they are to the real list.

7. Repeat the same activity, adding music or some other background noise.

8. Compare both lists and discuss the challenges with listening when there is extra noise.

9. Discuss the importance of listening to follow directions. Use the best list to make a project.

6.1C Brainstorming for a Topic

Time: 5–10 minutes

Purpose: Illustrate the importance of listening to each other in a group.

Materials: Worksheet 6.1 Brainstorming for a Group Project on page 208 in Appendix B, paper, pencils, idea for project

Preparation: Make copies of the worksheet.

Procedure:

1. Decide on a project for the children. Examples: puppet show, party, or play.
2. Break the children into groups of three to five. Have them move the groups to different areas in the room.
3. Describe the theme for the project.
4. Hand out the brainstorming sheets to each group.
5. Assign one child to write down all the ideas and then their final choice.
6. Let them go and observe their listening abilities while they brainstorm. Try to facilitate as little as possible. Redirect the children back to the group whenever possible.
7. Give them a countdown to finish.
8. Bring them back and ask them what they came up with. Questions to ask:
   a. Did anyone agree on a topic?
   b. What were some of the ideas?
   c. Who had trouble listening to the others?
   d. Why?
   e. Who didn't get heard?
   f. Why?
9. Develop a list as a group on how to help everyone listen when you are brainstorming ideas. (Refer back to original concept map.)
10. Use this list and idea for future group projects.

6.1D Friendship Cards—Appropriate Behavior in a Group

Time: 5–10 minutes

Purpose: The friendship cards are used as a visual reminder for the children to reinforce the concept that has been taught.

Materials: Friendship Cards in Appendix A:

- Interested Face
- Listening Body

Preparation: See directions in "How to Use This Book" on page 12.

Procedure: See directions in "How to Use This Book" on page 12.

Generalization and Consistency

- Directly requesting eye contact is the most successful method for strengthening eye contact when listening and explaining.
- Request for eye contact when the children are making statements or requesting objects.
- Put the emphasis on the fact that only when they look at the other person do they know that he or she is speaking or listening to them.
- Give positive feedback to the children when they show great listening skills by following directions or answering questions with appropriate answers.
- If the children are not successful in a game or activity, brainstorm ways for the children to increase their listening skills so that they will improve their success.

Lesson 6.2

Socializing With Peers in a Group

Introduction/Overview

To interact and work successfully in a group, a person needs to strengthen his or her ability to multitask. The skills that are used when multitasking are listening, focusing on the activity, positively interacting, and initiating interactions with others. The activities chosen for this lesson are dramatic play scenarios or group projects. If the children know and use the skills needed to be able to play with others in dramatic play settings, they will be able to be more successful in other group activities. It may be necessary to start with a dramatic play scenario and then, for the older children, use the group project activity after you have seen the children using the basic positive interaction skills in a group setting. It is helpful to refer to Unit 3: Social Skills for Interacting With Friends and the lessons that teach sweet/kind words to support positive interaction skills during group interactions.

Teaching Concepts

- Interacting with the group helps to make the activity fun.
- Being a part of a group activity requires many tasks, and learning the tasks makes being with others easier and more fun.
- Teaching group skills can be accomplished while playing with others in a group activity.

Attitudinal Approach

- Children can be more successful in group activities if taught the individual skills needed to play and interact in a group.
- Learning how to play in a group helps younger children learn the basic skills necessary to work in group activities when they are older.

- Sensitivity to all the skills needed and understanding that these skills can be taught and learned helps to increase a child's success in interacting.

Lesson Objectives

- Children will learn positive communication skills necessary to interact with others in a group.
- Children will learn to initiate interactions and get someone's attention in a group environment.
- Children will increase their ability to focus attention to other members of the group.

Lesson Introduction

Brainstorm for Key Concepts

Have children develop lists to refer to by asking specific questions. Use the directions found on page 11 in the "How to Use This Book" section. *Time:* 5–15 minutes

- What are the types of words we use when talking to our friends? List the sweet/kind words we have learned before when we talk to our friends.
- What are the words or phrases we can use to share ideas with our friends?
- How do we get people's attention when we want to talk to them?
- What can you do to help you to pay more attention to others when talking to them in a group?

Activities

6.2A Dramatic Play Center

Time: 10–20 minutes

Purpose: This group activity gives children the opportunity to interact with peers, use their imagination, use positive language, share, take turns, and initiate basic problem-solving ideas. This is also a great opportunity to observe the children's dramatic play skills and learn both their interaction strengths and challenges. This is the first activity to build group skills. Modify the toys or theme to fit the children's interest and age.

Materials: Dolls or toy figures; theme-based play scenario such as farm with animals, dollhouse, or castle with knights and princesses. Also have available additional toys such as blocks to offer for children to expand the play theme.

Preparation: Arrange a center area with enough space for the children to move around comfortably but blocked off so children will not wander away from the interaction. Have toys organized on shelves or in baskets so children can easily get to them and see what is available.

Procedure:

1. Introduce the play theme to the children.

2. Show the children all the toys available.

3. Make sure there are enough toys for each child to easily participate.

4. Observe the children's play and facilitate as needed. Make suggestions to children to expand the play scenario. Prompt positive language and facilitate any conflicts. Allow the children enough time to self-correct but then step in when needed. Refer to "Guidelines for Curriculum Success" for specific ideas.

6.2B Group Project

Time: 15–20 minutes per session

Purpose: This is the next step in helping children to successfully work in a group. Use the brainstorming sheets the children generated in Lesson 1: Listening in a Group. This is a multistep activity that may take a few sessions. It is beneficial to check in with children (individually if necessary) to note their participation and understanding. Tell the children that each child should have at least one task on the to-do list.

Materials: Group project brainstorm sheets from Lesson 1; Worksheet 6.2 Group Meeting Note (page 209) and Worksheet 6.3 Group Project To-Do List (page 210) in Appendix B

Preparation: Make copies of the worksheets.

Procedure:

1. Have children regroup into their brainstorming groups from the Listening in a Group lesson.

2. Have the children use the topic they decided on to begin planning the group project.

3. Explain how to use the "Group Project To-Do List" and "Group Meeting Notes" worksheets.

4. Allow the children as much independence as possible while planning their group project.

5. Check-ins with the children are extremely important, especially if you see any struggles or conflicts.

6. Check in with the group as a whole at the end of each session to ask for feedback about the group's progress. Use the worksheets that the children have filled out to ask specific questions about the project. The more specific the questions, the more likely it is they will get responses about the actual progress.

6.2C Friendship Cards—Appropriate Behavior in a Group

Time: 5–10 minutes

Purpose: The friendship cards are used as a visual reminder for the children to reinforce the concept that has been taught.

Materials: Friendship Cards in Appendix A:

- Words to Use When Sharing Ideas
- Ways to Get Someone's Attention

Preparation: See directions in "How to Use This Book" on page 12.

Procedure: See directions in "How to Use This Book" on page 12.

Generalization and Consistency

- When a child is interrupting others in a group setting, ask the child to wait until the present conversation is finished, and then he or she will have an opportunity to speak. Remind the child frequently that what he or she has to say is important and to please wait until it is his or her turn.
- When children raise their hands during instructions or directions, ask if they want to ask a question, make a comment, or tell a story. If it is a question, ask the child to wait until you give all the directions. If it is a comment or story, ask the child to wait till the activity begins, and then you will come to him or her and listen.
- When asking the children to contribute to a group discussion or when giving verbal directions, request their eye contact; state the question or direction slowly, giving specific clues; then wait for them to respond.
- Creating more opportunities for children have leadership roles and be invested in interaction will help them develop a comfort in being involved.
- Have a child's major role in an activity be a particular responsibility or decision-making role to strengthen her or his confidence.

Lesson 6.3

Learning in a Group

Introduction/Overview

The aspects of learning in a group correspond to the concepts of interacting in a group. The additional challenge that is added when the children are expected to learn in a group atmosphere includes the teaching of information that is new to the children and requires increased attention and focusing skills. Additional supports are often needed to meet a child's specific challenges. Use of visual supports or physical movement often increases a child's ability to learn. Also, many children have the ability to appear as if they are attending when they are not. Checking in is a necessity to make sure a child is retaining the information given. Practicing using additional supports and strategies will increase a child's ability to retain information in the future.

Teaching Concepts

- It is as much fun to learn with others as it is to learn on our own.
- If you get confused or are not sure of what to do, ask for help.
- Written directions can help you to follow along with the group activity.

Attitudinal Approach

- Learning in a group environment has many possible additional challenges.
- Children can benefit from increased visual support and more specific instructions to increase their ability to be successful in a group project.
- If a child is having trouble contributing to the group activity, adapting the activity for the child should always be done before behavior modification is attempted.

Lesson Objectives

- Children will learn skills to increase their attention to the activity.
- Children will learn to utilize visual supports offered to help participate in the group activity.
- Children will strengthen their ability to increase awareness of how to use their body in a group of friends.

Lesson Introduction

Concept Map—What Helps Us Learn in a Group?

Have the children help develop a concept map (see Figure 6.2) by asking leading questions. Use the directions found on page 11 in the "How to Use This Book" section. *Time:* 10–15 minutes

Figure 6.2 What Helps Us Learn in a Group Concept Map

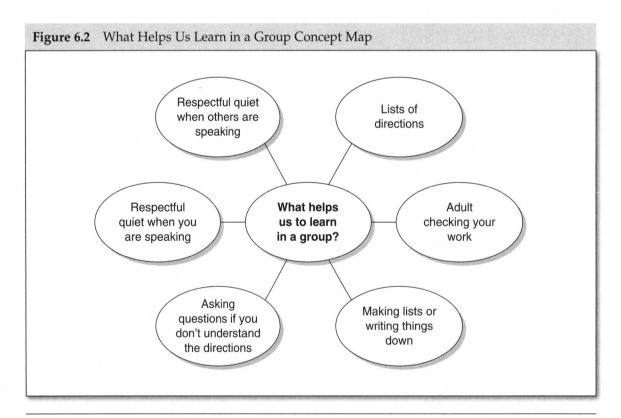

Activities

6.3A Clue Hunt

Time: 10–20 minutes

Purpose: This is a small-group activity that gives the children the opportunity to work together to find the answer with the clues that are hidden. The skills that should be reinforced include listening, using eye contact, positive language, focusing, impulse control, and body space awareness.

Materials: Clue Flashcards on page 213 in Appendix B

Preparation:

1. Photocopy clue cards.

2. Cut out clue cards

3. Color clue cards if you think additional visual support would increase the focusing ability of the children in your group.

Procedure:

1. Hide the three clues around the room. Have only three to five children per group. Two or more groups can be hunting for clues at the same time. Make sure the groups are separated enough so the children do not find each other's clues.

2. Explain that this is a group game, so the whole group is to try to figure out the answer as a group.

3. Once all three clues are found, have the children bring them to a table or specific area to begin thinking as a group about the answer.

4. The group needs to check with each member to agree on an answer before the group tells the facilitator the answer.

5. Once they figure out the answer, the children raise their hands to tell the facilitator the answer.

6. If they are correct, you can have the group hide their eyes while you hide more clues.

7. If the group is wrong, tell them to try to think as a group again for the answer.

6.3B Goop Project

Time: 10–20 minutes

Purpose: This group activity can be adapted to use any simple recipe. We chose goop because the end result gives sensory input and feels really cool. Keep in mind that the feeling of the goop may be too challenging for some children. The focus of this activity is to use a simple recipe and to allow a small group of children to work together to make something.

Materials: A copy of Worksheet 6.4 Goop on page 211 in Appendix B for each group of children (pictures can be added to the written directions for the beginning readers to increase independence); ingredients listed in the recipe, clearly labeled; measuring utensils, mixing bowls, spoons, individual containers

Preparation: Adapt recipe if necessary, make copies of recipe, and assemble supplies and utensils.

Procedure:

1. Assemble children into small groups

2. Explain activity. Read recipe and use the supplies as visual support when describing the activity.

3. Have children "make the goop." Try to allow as much independence as possible.

4. When the children have finished, allow them time to explore the goop as a group, or pour it into individual containers.

6.3C "Swimmy" Book Project   *Time:* 15–30 minutes

Purpose: This activity combines using a story that teaches positive friendship skills with a group activity to help generalize the group skills taught in the lesson introduction.

Materials: **Swimmy** by Leo Lionni, large roll of paper, small paper plates, scissors, stapler, red and blue paint, glue

Preparation: Assemble supplies. Draw large fish outline on poster. Cut out a small triangle in the plate (the mouth) and staple this to the other side of the plate (as the tail).

Procedure:

1. Read book to children.

2. Have children paint the poster blue around the fish.

3. Have children paint the fish red.

4. Paint one fish black.

5. Glue small fish onto poster inside the outline of the big fish. Fill this whole area with red fish.

6. Use the black fish in the space where the eye of the big fish should be.

7. When finished, review with the children the friendship skills that are used by the fish in the story.

6.3D Friendship Cards—Appropriate Behavior in a Group

Time: 5–10 minutes

Purpose: The friendship cards are used as a visual reminder for the children to reinforce the concept that has been taught.

Materials: Friendship Card in Appendix A: Ways We Learn in a Group

Preparation: See directions in "How to Use This Book" on page 12.

Procedure: See directions in "How to Use This Book" on page 12.

Generalization and Consistency

- When a child gets distracted, help with recall and developing focus by restating the directions instead of tell the child to stop what she or he is doing.
- Use redirecting phrases such as "Remember the directions," "What should you be doing now?" or "What did I say were the directions?"
- If any children benefit from the visual supports used, generalize this strategy in other environments to help them attend and focus better.

Lesson 6.4

Following Directions in Groups

Introduction/Overview

In classroom settings, all children will have some experience in an adult-led group. The objective of this is to develop their ability to attend in a meaningful way to the interactive nuances. Without proper instruction on the skills needed to attend in groups, children can easily get lost in the flow of the interaction. This sense of confusion can frustrate a child and often can lead to inappropriate behaviors in group settings. With proper instruction and practice, children are able to be productive members of groups and have rich learning experiences.

Teaching Concepts

- We learn from the information we gather from groups.
- Group settings are good environments for us to share our ideas.
- We learn from others.

Attitudinal Approach

- The length of the circle time/meeting time should be based on the children's attention span, not our lesson plan.
- Sensory input is a necessity for all children to be successful.
- Integrating visual, verbal, experiential, repetitious, and kinesthetic learning should be imbedded in all circle and meeting times.

Lesson Objectives

- Children will strengthen their ability to attend for extended durations.
- Children will follow teaching themes in a group setting.
- Children will raise hands, take turns, and participate appropriately in a group setting.

Lesson Introduction

Concept Map—Circle Time/Meeting Time

Have the children help develop a concept map (see Figure 6.3) by asking leading questions. Use the directions found on page 11 in the "How to Use This Book" section. *Time:* 5–10 minutes

Figure 6.3 Circle Time/Meeting Time Concept Map

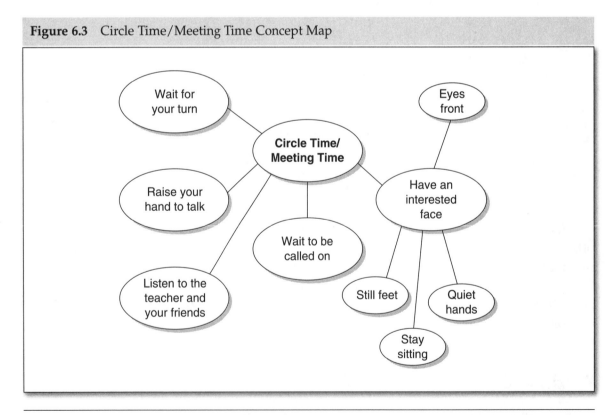

Activities

6.4A Draw an Interested Face

Time: 10–15 minutes

Purpose: This activity will build awareness in the children of not only how to increase their attention and listening but also how to look more interested while attending.

Materials: Worksheet 6.5 Interested Face on page 212 in Appendix B, mirror, markers, crayons

Preparation: Make copies of face outline and assemble supplies.

Procedure:

1. While children are looking in the mirror, have them practice making interested faces.

2. Split the children into pairs and have one child draw the other child making an interested face.

3. When finished, switch so the other child has the opportunity to draw.

4. Share the pictures with the group when finished.

6.4B I Am Going on a Picnic

Time: 5–15 minutes

Purpose: Children follow a play theme and attend to conversation in a group setting.

Materials: Use a ball or visual cue to help children understand whose turn it is.

Preparation: None

Procedure:

1. The adult goes first and says, "I am going on a picnic, and I am going to bring (something that begins with the letter A—e.g., apples)."

2. The next person says the same thing adding something with the letter B. ("I am going on a picnic, and I am going to bring apples and bananas.")

3. Continue the game until someone cannot remember the order. That child gets to start the next round.

4. We suggest that no one is considered out in this game. Continue to give the children the opportunity to attend.

6.4C Outburst Jr. by Parker Brothers

Time: 10–20 minutes

Purpose: Strengthen children's focus and control in an exciting activity.

Materials: Outburst Jr. by Parker Brothers

Preparation: None

Procedure:

1. Play game per the instructions with the modification of children needing to raise their hand in order to guess.

2. Alternate between allowing children to yell out for one round and having children raise their hands for another.

3. Discuss the pros and cons of playing both ways.

6.4D Friendship Cards—Appropriate Behavior in a Group

Time: 5–10 minutes

Purpose: The friendship cards are used as a visual reminder for the children to reinforce the concept that has been taught.

Materials: Friendship Card in Appendix A: Circle Time/Meeting Time

Preparation: See directions in "How to Use This Book" on page 12.

Procedure: See directions in "How to Use This Book" on page 12.

Generalization and Consistency

- When children raise their hands during instructions or directions, ask if they want to ask a question, make a comment, or tell a story. If it is a question, ask the child to wait till you give all the directions. If it is a comment or story, ask the child to wait till the activity begins, and then you will come to him or her and listen.
- Offer adult-directed opportunities where the children are redirected back to the activity and reassure them of when they will have their choice.

UNIT 7

Playing Games

In this unit, we work on appropriate play in a variety of settings. So many of the children we work with have difficulty in play situations due to a lack of knowledge of how to play. In this lesson, we are attempting to help the children develop play vocabulary and practice the interactive skills needed for interactive play.

SOCIAL GOALS

- Child will use appropriate language and attitude when playing.
- Child will identify what sportsmanship is and use it in a play setting.
- Child will be able to suggest and use a method of figuring out who goes first fairly.
- Child will play appropriate indoor games and activities.
- Child will be able to identify and exercise safely during outdoor play.
- Child will be able to play video games interactively with others in different environments.

 Lesson 7.1

Sportsmanship/Cheering and Encouragement

Introduction/Overview

Many of the times we see conflicts between children in a play situation, it is because they are using negative language and attitudes toward each other. Almost always this happens when one child is not doing things the way their friends want to do things. Most children have been exposed to so much negative response in these types of situation that it is the only way they know to react to their frustration. This is where the conflict happens. Instead of using positive language to support others, they use criticizing and aggressive tones. In this lesson, we teach children how to encourage each other during play and to use positive sportsmanship at the end of games.

Teaching Concepts

- We cheer for our friends to show that we like them.
- We give encouragement before, during, and after.
- Cheering helps us as well as others who are playing.
- We are supportive when friends win.
- We encourage others when we win.
- We play positive or we don't play.

Attitudinal Approach

- Adults need to overexaggerate our cheering to help children see how big it should be.
- It is difficult to see past losing to encourage the win, and this might take some time.
- There is no reason to feel bad about not winning.

Lesson Objectives

- Children will identify the different ways to cheer their friends.
- Children will list the times and places to encourage others.
- Children will list the benefits of being supportive of friends.
- Children will practice cheering for each other in a game.

Lesson Introduction

Brainstorm for Key Concepts

Have children develop lists to refer to by asking specific questions. Use the directions found on page 11 in the "How to Use This Book" section. *Time:* 10–15 minutes.

- Define "sportsmanship" or "being a good sport."
- Play a game so everyone enjoys it.
- List of encouragement/cheers.
- Brainstorm when we should use these cheers.
- Different places to encourage/cheer.
- Why we encourage/cheer.

Activities

7.1A Copy the
Design/Best the Time

Time: 5–10 minutes

Purpose: In this game the children are asked to work as a group under a time pressure. In a situation like this, unsportsmanlike language is usually used out of frustration.

Materials: Worksheet 7.1 Copy the Picture on page 217 in Appendix B, markers

Preparation: Copy the worksheets so there are enough for each child to have two or three.

Procedure:

1. Separate children into two teams or into pairs.

2. Give each child a paper with a silly design on it.

3. Give each team/pair one marker to share.

4. When the timer starts, the children can copy or trace the silly designs. When they are done, they pass the marker to the next person.

5. Encourage the children to use the cheers they had brainstormed to help their friends.

6. Try the game again with everyone being silent.

7. Discuss with the children which way they liked better. Find out which was more fun. Point out the time it took for each and discuss the difference.

7.1B Friend Fan Poster

Time: 15–20 minutes

Purpose: In this activity, children create a poster that is in support of a friend.

Materials: Poster or large paper for each child, markers and art supplies

Preparation: Start activity by having children brainstorm what things they would put on a poster for a local sports hero if they were going to see him or her play.

Procedure:

1. Get the children into pairs. Extra challenge: For older groups, pick children's names out of a hat to make pairs so that they are making posters for people they spend less time with. Make sure to prompt the children about "sweet words" and positive language and emphasize that the goal is to encourage a friend.

2. Have children share something that they like about the friend they are paired with or why she or he is a good sport. (If children are picking out of a hat, use this time as an open question time where children can ask their partner questions to get to know what game she or he likes to play and what strengths to cheer for.)

3. Ask each child to pretend that the friend is involved in a sports game and that he or she is going to cheer for that friend.

4. Using markers and poster board, have each child make a poster to cheer for that friend.

5. Have each child share the poster that she or he made about the friend.

7.1C Obstacle
Course/Beat the Time

Time: 10–15 minutes

Purpose: This is a gross motor game that challenges the children's ability to use positive sportsmanship. Here there is the pressure of a time constraint that challenges the children's ability to stay calm and not use negative language with peers who are slower or more challenged.

Materials: Gross motor equipment or furniture

Preparation: Set up an obstacle course in a safe space.

Procedure:

1. This activity can be done as a large group or by splitting the class in teams of two.

2. Have the group(s) go through the obstacle course and time how long it takes for all of the students to complete the course.

3. Go through the course again, and this time have the children cheer each member of the group as she or he goes through.

4. Compare times and discuss how it felt when others were cheering for you. Point out if any children were choosing negative comments and ask children to discuss if that is effective in supporting a teammate.

5. Game modification: Use the same procedure for a relay race situation if space is limited or children are too old for obstacle courses. Races such as balancing a cotton ball on a spoon, a balloon under the chin, or a playground ball between the knees are challenging and add a silly aspect to keep things fun.

7.1D Friendship Cards—
Playing Games

Time: 5–10 minutes

Purpose: The friendship cards are used as a visual reminder for the children to reinforce the concept that has been taught.

Materials: Friendship Cards in Appendix A:

- A Good Sport
- Ways to Cheer Your Friends

Preparation: See directions in "How to Use This Book" on page 12.

Procedure: See directions in "How to Use This Book" on page 12.

Generalization and Consistency

- Hang brainstorming list and encouragement posters in the classroom and refer to them before competitive activities or if the children forget to use positive encouragement.

Lesson 7.2

Going First

Introduction/Overview

Over the years, we have been surprised at how often we have come across children who had no idea how to figure out in a fair way who would go first. It amazed us how many times children would go back and forth saying "I want to go first" and never realize that that was not creating a solution for them. In this lesson, we introduce the ways of figuring out who goes first and explore the importance of not always going first.

Teaching Concepts

- Figuring out who goes first is something we do fairly.
- Going first is not always important.
- We can win if we go second, third, or fourth.

Attitudinal Approach

- The thrill of going first is very enticing and very difficult to let go.
- Many children have not been taught how to figure out who goes first.

Lesson Objectives

- Children will identify different fair ways to figure out who goes first.
- Children will have the experience of trying a new way to learn to go first.
- Children will accept others going first calmly.

Lesson Introduction

Brainstorm for Key Concepts

Have children develop lists to refer to by asking specific questions. Use the directions found on page 11 in the "How to Use This Book" section. *Time:* 10–15 minutes.

Ways to Figure Out Who Goes First

- Evens/odds
- Flip a coin
- Guess the number
- One potato
- Roll the highest number (dice or spinner)
- Bubble gum, bubble gum
- Einy-Meeny-Miney-Moe

- Pick numbers out of a hat
- Draw straws
- Birthday person or person with closest birthday
- Youngest to oldest
- Tallest to shortest
- Draw names out of a hat
- Rock/paper/scissors

Activities

7.2A Practice and Learn a New One   *Time:* 5–10 minutes

Purpose: Introduce children to new techniques for going first and discuss what to do if they don't get a chance to go first and how to deal with it.

Materials: Large paper for brainstorming, copies of Worksheet 7.2 Who Goes First? on page 218 in Appendix B for each group

Preparation: Choose a way to figure out who goes first. Make copies for the directions for the technique if appropriate for the children.

Procedure:

1. After the children make the list of the Ways to Figure Out Who Goes First, introduce a new way to figure out who goes first.

2. Split the children in to groups of four and have them practice the new way. Have them use the technique five or six times and make a list of who was selected to go first.

3. Come together as a group and discuss how many times each person got to go first and brainstorm as a group what to do if someone does not get a chance to go first.

7.2B Short Game Stations   *Time:* 10–15 minutes

Purpose: This is a great opportunity for children to practice figuring out who goes first. The object is to make it about the different ways of going first and not the game itself.

Materials: Short games that take only a few minutes to play such as tic-tac-toe, Jenga, or Topple; timer

Preparation: Set up stations in different parts of the class so that only a few children can be at one game at a time.

Procedure:

1. Describe the games and tell the children that they are going to play different games at each station. Let children know that they may not finish the games. This is just a time to practice figuring out who goes first.

2. Have children stay at each station for 3 to 5 minutes or enough time for them to figure out who goes first and to play a game.

3. Get together at the end and ask the children's opinion on what method is best for figuring out who goes first.

7.2C Friendship Cards— Playing Games

Time: 5–10 minutes

Purpose: The friendship cards are used as a visual reminder for the children to reinforce the concept that has been taught.

Materials: Friendship Card in Appendix A: Ways to Figure Out Who Goes First

Preparation: See directions in "How to Use This Book" on page 12.

Procedure: See directions in "How to Use This Book" on page 12.

Generalization and Consistency

- When children are having a challenge remembering the strategies used, refer them back to their pack of friendship cards.
- Hang posters and concept maps and refer to them before children begin competitive games.

Lesson 7.3

Who Won?

Introduction/Overview

How we treat others in the face of winning and losing is at the heart of many of the conflicts that children have when playing competitive games. Many children get their feelings hurt when someone else wins a game, and some are ridiculed if they win. In this lesson, we discuss the way we treat others when we win and what we say and do if someone else wins. It is important to help the children to see that having fun and challenging ourselves are the main goals of any game.

Teaching Concepts

- We play games to have fun.
- Being a good sport is how we end a game.

Attitudinal Approach

- The thrill of competing is as good if not better than winning itself.
- Children might need help seeing the positive outcomes when someone else wins.
- Winning is exciting and difficult to see past.

Lesson Objectives

- Children will identify and use positive phrases and attitudes with their peers when they win a game.
- Children will identify and use positive phrases and attitudes with their peers when someone else wins a game.

Lesson Introduction

Concept Map—Who Won?

Have the children help develop a concept map by asking leading questions (see Figure 7.1). Use the directions found on page 11 in the "How to Use This Book" section. *Time:* 10–15 minutes.

Suggested Questions

- Why do we play games?
- At the end of the game:
  - o What do we say when we are the winner?
  - o What do we say when someone else wins?
  - o How do we say it?

Activities

7.3A Try Trophy

Time: 10–15 minutes

Purpose: In this activity, we are emphasizing the importance of doing our best instead of winning.

Materials: Pint milk cartons, paper cups, pipe cleaners, construction paper, art supplies

Preparation: Cut the tops off the milk cartons. Wrap the milk cartons in construction paper.

Figure 7.1   Who Won Concept Map

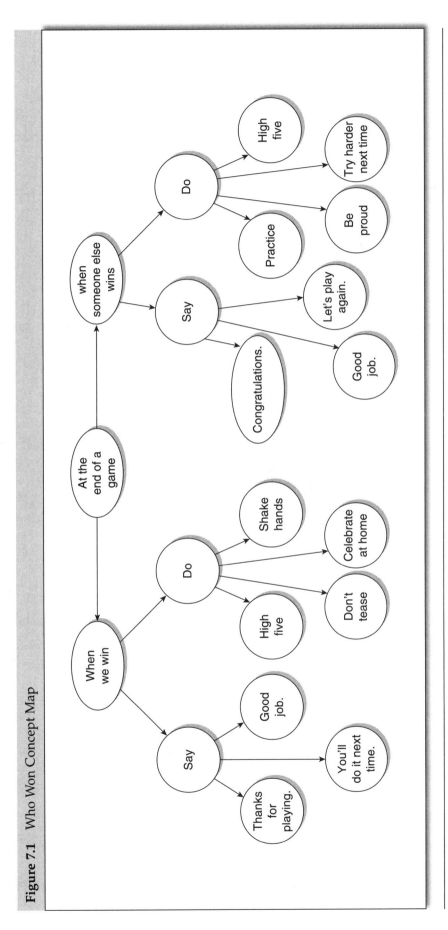

Procedure:

1. Have children glue the paper cups on the top of their milk cartons.

2. Use pipe cleaners to make handles of the trophy.

3. Have each child write something (or write it for them) that they consider their strength when playing games. Add their name (glitter makes the name stand out).

4. Have children decorate with stickers, markers, and other art materials.

5. After trophies are dry, display or have award ceremony of strengths to build self-esteem.

7.3B Friendship Cards— Playing Games

Time: 5–10 minutes

Purpose: The friendship cards are used as a visual reminder for the children to reinforce the concept that has been taught.

Materials: Friendship Cards in Appendix A:

- What We Say When We Win
- What We Say When Someone Else Wins

Preparation: See directions in "How to Use This Book" on page 12.

Procedure: See directions in "How to Use This Book" on page 12.

Lesson 7.4

Playing Friends' Games

Introduction/Overview

Many children become very rigid in the games they play. Not only that, but they want to play the games the same way over and over. In this lesson, we help children see the benefit of playing other people's games and playing them other ways. We help them to internalize the concept by showing them how much they benefit from playing friends' games.

Teaching Concepts

- Everyone has good ideas for games.
- It is fun to try new games and activities.
- We can try other people's things and still have it our way some of the time.

Attitudinal Approach

- Many children are rigid because they are overwhelmed in a situation.
- Children develop misconceptions about how things "should" be done.

Lesson Objectives

- Children will try new activities with peers.
- Children will teach peers new games that they enjoy.

Lesson Introduction

Brainstorm for Key Concepts

Have children develop lists to refer to by asking specific questions. Use the directions found on page 11 in the "How to Use This Book" section. *Time:* 10–15 minutes.

- What games do you like to play?
- What games do we like to play with friends?
- Why do we want to play games with friends?
- Sometimes we don't want to play the other game. Why don't we want to?

Activities

7.4A The Games We Like Collage   *Time:* 10–15 minutes

Purpose: This activity is to help the children get comfortable with the idea of playing other people's games. Many children get the idea that playing other people's games means that they do not get to play their own.

Materials: Large paper, toy catalogs, scissors, glue, markers

Preparation: Label a poster or large paper "Games I Like."

Procedure:

1. Share with the children that many times people like to play the same game and their friend will want to play something that they will like.

2. Have children go through toy catalogs and make a collage of the games and toys they like.

3. Have each child show the poster he or she made.

4. Have the children switch the posters (in pairs) and take turns pointing out the games and toys on their friend's poster they like too.

7.4B Change the Rules

Time: 5–10 minutes

Purpose: Children's rigidity can go as deep as the specific rules in a game. Some people call it "base," and others call it "home." This activity is designed to help children be okay with little changes and understand that it does not change the fun of the game.

Materials: Have children bring their favorite game from home. Request of parents that the game be short (can be played in 5 to 10 minutes).

Preparation: None

Procedure:

1. If working with a large group, split children into small groups of three or four.

2. Have one child explain the rules of her or his game to the rest of the group.

3. Everyone plays the game.

4. Then have each child, starting with the child who brought the game, think about one rule that they can change. Write the rules down to help them remember.

5. Play the game again.

6. After the game, talk about the game and the way the rules made it new and fun. Have children share which way is better. Remind them that rules can be changed, and then changed back as often as you want, as long as everyone agrees.

7. Go through the process again with another child's game.

7.4C Everyone Pick a Game and Make a List of Order

Time: 15–20 minutes

Purpose: In this activity, each child gets an opportunity to play "their game" and share it with friends. It also reinforces that other people's games are great to play and explore.

Materials: Games children bring from home

Preparation: Make a schedule with the children that outlines whose turn it is to bring a game in from home. For larger groups, split the children into share groups of four or five.

Procedure:

1. Each child will bring in a game from home or pick one from the class.

2. Have the children be in charge of explaining how the game is played to the other children.

3. Use the techniques for picking the child who goes first and for happy endings.

4. After the game is played, have children share what they liked about the game.

7.4D Friendship Cards— Playing Games

Time: 5–10 minutes

Purpose: The friendship cards are used as a visual reminder for the children to reinforce the concept that has been taught.

Materials: Friendship Card in Appendix A: Why We Play Friends' Games

Preparation: See directions in "How to Use This Book" on page 12.

Procedure: See directions in "How to Use This Book" on page 12.

Generalization and Consistency

- Use picture schedules with pictures of the children in some group play times where each child gets a turn picking the toy or game for the group. Pictures help children see that they will get their toy and their turn and make it easier for them to accept others' games.
- Refer children to the posters of why we play other people's games to help them remember what they can from the experience of trying a new game.
- Refer children to the poster of what they like to play, and have them pick toys and games that everyone enjoys.

Lesson 7.5

Outside Games

Introduction/Overview

At some time, all children will have an opportunity to play some active game. In this lesson, we go over the play vocabulary involved in outside games and sports and the body safety that is needed to make sure that all players have a fun and safe play time. One thing we suggest is creating a global policy about picking teams. To help children create positive attitudes about involving people regardless of ability, we suggest that you *do not allow children to have captains pick teams.* There are few people who do not have a negative experience about picking teams. We suggest eliminating this from your environment, especially if children are consistently having conflict over the process. Introduce the techniques in the first lesson as being better ways to create teams.

Teaching Concepts

- Active games are great for everyone.
- Teamwork and good sportsmanship are the most important parts of sports.
- Even observers are a part of a sports game.
- Sport safety is essential.
- Everybody is included and has fun.

Attitudinal Approach

- Everyone can be a part of the action.

Lesson Objectives

- Children will participate in sport and active games in a group setting.
- Children will try a new aspect of active games.

Lesson Introduction

Brainstorm for Key Concepts

Have children develop lists to refer to by asking specific questions. Use the directions found on page 11 in the "How to Use This Book" section. *Time:* 10–15 minutes.

- Brainstorm types of sports games.
- Brainstorm outdoor safety rules.

Activities

7.5A Positive Team Picking
Time: 5–10 minutes

Purpose: In this activity, we are helping children to build positive alternatives for picking teams that include all children. The purpose is to introduce the children to new techniques for picking teams and to discuss what to do if they do not get a chance to go first and how to deal with it.

Materials: Two pieces of large paper for brainstorming, posters or art paper, art supplies

Preparation: None

Procedure:

1. Start by discussing with the children how it feels to be left out of a game.

2. Have children brainstorm a list of ways to create teams without having captains picking.

3. Count off by twos.

4. Pick papers from a hat.

5. Split children into groups or have children work individually. Have children create posters about including all friends in games. Have children include one of the suggestions in the poster.

6. Hang posters and refer to them on a daily basis.

7.5B Soccer

Time: 15–20 minutes

Purpose: This is a good game to teach children. The rules can be simplified for any age and limitation. It is also helpful for creating body strength and muscle tone.

Materials: Soccer ball, something to use as goals, Worksheet 7.3 Scorecard A (page 219) or Worksheet 7.4 Scorecard B (page 220) in Appendix B depending on how many children are playing

Preparation: Set up field.

Procedure:

1. Have children play some as practice, stopping the game frequently to give pointers and suggestions.

2. After children practice, split into teams and begin keeping score.

3. At the end of the game, take the opportunity to review happy endings and use the skills they were introduced to in the lesson.

7.5C Making Baskets— Indoor/Outdoor HORSE

Time: 10–15 minutes

Purpose: Many games or simple outdoor interactions involve making baskets. It can be a source of anxiety for children who do not have the experience doing it. Practice is the only way to develop the ability to shoot baskets and is worth encouraging children to do. HORSE is a simple game that encourages children to go at their own speed and can be played in teams with the object of the entire team finishing.

Materials: Basketball—for indoors, laundry basket—and papers that have the letters for the word *horse* written on them

Preparation: Around a basketball hoop outdoors, put the letters on the ground at a distance appropriate for the children. Indoors, set desks in a circle around the laundry basket and put the letters on top of the desks.

Procedure:

1. Explain the rules of the game and assist the children in playing. If indoors, have children stand behind the desks or sit on top.

2. Split children into teams and set a goal of the whole team finishing to lengthen the game for less skilled shooters.

3. Encourage children to play HORSE on the playground in their free time to practice their skill.

7.5D Relay Race

Time: 10–15 minutes

Purpose: This is an activity that was used in the past, but it is very relevant to this unit, so we suggest using it again. This can be a good time to also do the challenge relay race again to point out the need to change games to meet friends' physical needs.

Materials: Spoons, golf balls, pom-pom balls, balloons

Preparation: Have children split into groups. Set up course.

Procedure:

1. Have children run relay races.

2. Each child needs to run out and back with the ball on the spoon without dropping the ball. If anyone drops the ball, he or she has to start over.

3. Start with the heaviest ball (it will stay on the spoon the best).

4. With each race, introduce a new ball or the balloon.

5. Remind the children they need to pay attention to their bodies and comment if someone becomes too crazy or wild and needs to gain some control.

6. Also point out when someone is going too slowly and can speed up.

7.5E Friendship Cards— Playing Games

Time: 5–10 minutes

Purpose: The friendship cards are used as a visual reminder for the children to reinforce the concept that has been taught.

Materials: Friendship Card in Appendix A: Ways to Be Safe Outside

Preparation: See directions in "How to Use This Book" on page 12.

Procedure: See directions in "How to Use This Book" on page 12.

Generalization and Consistency

- Refer children to friendship cards when they are having conflicts.
- Plan times of being on the playground or outdoor play setting to facilitate children and make sure the skills taught are being implemented.

Lesson 7.6

Indoor Games

Introduction/Overview

It benefits all children to develop a love of board games. Board and card games are the best way to help children develop interactive skills such as sharing, waiting for a turn, communicating, and conflict resolution. Traditionally, dramatic play is usually only addressed in the early childhood years. We chose to include this in our elementary curriculum because for many children there are deficiencies in playing pretend that go unnoticed until well into kindergarten and continue to be a challenge through first to third grade, where children still dabble in the dramatics. In this unit, we try to reinforce the children's understanding of playing pretend and set up dramatic scenes for children to practice with others. Many children with special needs are concrete thinkers and are drawn to building and construction. They can, however, have difficulty with the social needs in these types of situations. In this lesson, we introduce the children to the vocabulary and safety issues when working with others on construction projects.

Teaching Concepts

- There are many rules in board games that make them fun and challenging.
- Everyone must agree to the rules to play the game.
- Communicating verbally is the key to avoiding conflicts with others.

Attitudinal Approach

- Children may have difficulty with self-control in open play and need patience to help them work out conflicts.
- It is easy for children to get overwhelmed with the sensory stimulation in open play indoors, and they will need sensory input.

Lesson Objectives

- Children will interact with peers in a safe way in a variety of indoor games.
- Children will come up with dramatic play themes with peers.
- Children will play board games appropriately.

Lesson Introduction

Brainstorm for Key Concepts

Have children develop lists to refer to by asking specific questions. Use the directions found on page 11 in the "How to Use This Book" section. *Time:* 10–15 minutes.

- What do we play indoors?
- How do we play board games?
- How do we have fun with friends in pretend play?
- How do we build safely?

Activities

7.6A Restaurant Dramatic Play

Time: 10–15 minutes

Purpose: This activity may be too young for children who are in the elementary grades, but it should still be considered as an option. Pretend play is difficult for some children who are concrete thinkers to grasp. Dramatic play experiences are wonderful opportunities for working on relating to others, social language, and problem-solving skills.

Materials: Play food, dishes, paper and art supplies, costumes, space with tables and chairs

Preparation: If necessary, brainstorm with the children the things you see in a restaurant and make a sequence of what happens when you go to a restaurant (see Figure 7.2) using Worksheet 7.5 What Happens Next on page 221 in Appendix B.

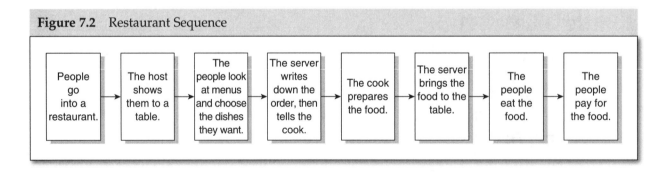

Figure 7.2 Restaurant Sequence

People go into a restaurant. → The host shows them to a table. → The people look at menus and choose the dishes they want. → The server writes down the order, then tells the cook. → The cook prepares the food. → The server brings the food to the table. → The people eat the food. → The people pay for the food.

Procedure:

1. Have children pick who they want to be.

2. Facilitate by staying back and observing and suggesting idea when the play starts to slow.

3. If children are extremely challenged, take a role in the play and model how to be involved and pretend to be a part.

7.6B Building Challenge

Time: 10–15 minutes

Purpose: In this challenge, the children are asked to work together with building materials and interact with other children in a safe way. The skills needed for building and construction in group settings are used throughout the school years in classroom projects.

Materials: Building materials, plastic cup, small blocks or marbles to use as weights in the cup

Preparation: Review the rules with the children that were introduced in the safe body lesson in Unit 3. Brainstorm a list of things that we also need to remember to keep our bodies safe when playing with building materials.

- Keep materials on the floor or table (no throwing).
- Hand things to our friends.
- Watch our hands and feet so we do not knock things over.
- Ask before we knock someone's project down.

Procedure:

1. Split children into groups and distribute building materials so all groups have about the same amount.

2. Tell the children that they need to build a tower that is very strong and can support the weight of the plastic cup with the weights inside.

3. Observe the children as they build, facilitating the children through different conflicts.

4. At the end of the game, warn the children that the buildings might fall, and if they do you will help them rebuild. Put the cup on the top of each building and add a set amount of weights into the cup to see if it can support it. After each building is tested, ask the children if they want to see how much the buildings can hold until they fall down. (Note: Do not suggest this if any of the children have difficulties about construction falling down.)

5. Extra challenge: Add a height requirement to the instructions, such as that the construction must be at least 1 foot high and support the weight.

7.6C Life-Size Board Game

Time: 15–20 minutes

Purpose: This is a great activity for helping children with the directional aspect of board games. Physically creating the game and acting it out helps children internalize the aspects of board game playing. It is great to leave this game out as a center in the classroom after the game is created so children can continue to play at different times.

Materials: Polyspots, index cards, pint milk cartons, markers

Preparation: Wrap milk cartons in white paper.

Procedure:

1. Brainstorm rules for board games

2. Have children brainstorm the different things that can happen in a board game when you land on a particular spot (examples: go ahead two spaces, go back two spaces, take another turn, lose a turn).

3. Have children lay out polyspots in a path with a start and an end and color dots on the milk cartons to make dice.

4. Write the directions that the children brainstormed on cards and have them tape them on the "board." Include a "start," a "finish," and cards with arrows drawn on them to help children with direction of play.

5. Have children put the cards on to make the game. Using the dice, play with the children as the pieces of the game.

7.6D Create Your Own Board Game

Time: 20–25 minutes

Purpose: Similar to the life-size board game, this activity will give children a hands-on experience with the ins and outs of board game playing.

Materials: Old board game, art materials, materials needed for the specific parts of the game based on the children's brainstorming, Worksheet 6.1 Brainstorming for a Group Project on page 208 in Appendix B

Preparation:

1. Glue paper on the top of the board game to cover its original artwork.

2. Help children build an awareness of the different parts of the board game by starting with a concept map.

Concept Map—What Are the Parts of a Board Game?

Have the children help develop a concept map by asking leading questions (see Figure 7.3). Use the directions found in the "How to Use This Book" section.

Figure 7.3 What Are the Parts of a Board Game Concept Map

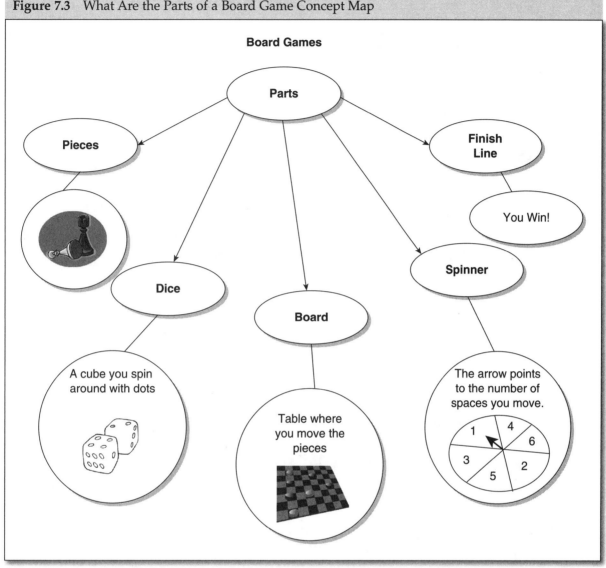

Procedure:

1. As a group, have the children think of a theme for the game. Encourage them to be as crazy and creative as they can. Decide number of players; the theme; whether to use dice (and how many) or a spinner, or both; and so on.

2. Split the group into teams to work on the different parts of the game. Have the children use the brainstorming project sheet to help them plan what they need to do to create the section of the game they are responsible for.

3. Based on the brainstorming, collect the materials needed. Suggestions: clay for creating the game pieces, wood blocks for dice, paper plates for spinners, and so forth.

4. Work on project with check-ups on the children as they progress.

5. When game is finished, have the children play in teams. This is good time to add to the centers.

7.6E Centers

Time: 15–20 minutes

Purpose: The purpose of the centers is to set up a natural environment where the children are exploring play together. This is a wonderful culmination activity for children to use all they have learned.

Materials: Materials and toys available

Preparation: Set up a space that has table-top games, building, dramatic play, art, and reading.

Procedure:

1. Have planned time in the day where children can interact in the centers and can be supported by an adult. This is the time to allow children some extra time to try the skills taught and even to allow them to use the wrong strategy, giving them the opportunity to self-correct.

7.6F Friendship Cards— Playing Games

Time: 5–10 minutes

Purpose: The friendship cards are used as a visual reminder for the children to reinforce the concept that has been taught.

Materials: Friendship Card in Appendix A: Parts of a Board Game

Preparation: See directions in "How to Use This Book" on page 12.

Procedure: See directions in "How to Use This Book" on page 12.

Generalization and Consistency

- Post rules.
- Refer children to friendship cards when they are having conflicts.
- Remember the importance of planned, structured, facilitated play days.

Appendix A

Friendship Cards

Master List

Unit 1—Discovering Social Skills

- Friendship
- Why Friends Are Great
- Ways to Say Hello
- Ways to Introduce Yourself
- Ways to Show Appreciation
- Things We Can Find Out About Friends
- Our Friends
- How Our Friends Act

Unit 2—Using Appropriate Eye Contact for Interaction

- Why We Look at Other People
- Why Other People Look at Us
- Where We Look When We Are Talking
- Why We Look at the Eyes When We Are Talking
- How Looking Helps Us to Listen
- What We Learn From Looking
- What We Do With Others
- Why We Have Friends

Unit 3—Social Skills for Interacting With Friends

- What You Do to Be a Good Friend
- Sweet Words You Can Use
- Why We Use Sweet/Kind Words With Our Friends
- Why We Keep Our Bodies Safe

- Why We Keep Our Friends' Bodies Safe
- How We Use Our Hands/Feet
- How We Use Our Bodies
- What We Do Together to Play and Have Fun

Unit 4—Appropriate Body Behavior

- My Personal Space
- What We Say if Someone Is in Our Personal Space
- Things I Do Well
- Things I Need Help With
- People Who Help Me
- Things We Do to Respect Our Friends' Body Privacy
- What I Do if Someone Invades My Body Privacy
- What We Do in the Morning to Be Neat and Clean
- What We Do During the Day to Be Neat and Clean
- What We Do at Night to Be Neat and Clean
- How We Slow Our Body When It Is Too Fast
- How We Get Our Body Moving When It Is Too Slow
- Places for Fast Body Speed
- Places for Slow Body Speed
- Places for Focused Body

153

Unit 5—Appropriate Emotional Behavior

- Emotions I Know
- Ways to Stay Calm
- How to Share My Emotions

Unit 6 – Appropriate Behavior in a Group

- Interested Face
- Listening Body
- Words to Use When Sharing Ideas
- Ways to Get Someone's Attention

- Ways We Learn in a Group
- Circle Time/Meeting Time

Unit 7—Playing Games

- A Good Sport
- Ways to Cheer Your Friends
- Ways to Figure Out Who Goes First
- What We Say When We Win
- What We Say When Someone Else Wins
- Why We Play Friends' Games
- Ways to Be Safe Outside
- Parts of a Board Game

the
WANNA PLAY
program
This pack of friendship cards belongs to:

_____

Unit 1 – Discovering Social Skills
Friendship

❖

❖

❖

the
WANNA PLAY
program

Unit 1 – Discovering Social Skills
Why Friends Are Great

❖

❖

❖

the
WANNA PLAY
program

Unit 1 – Discovering Social Skills
Ways to Say Hello

❖

❖

❖

the
WANNA PLAY
program

Unit 1 – Discovering Social Skills
Ways to Introduce Yourself

❖

❖

❖

the
WANNA PLAY
program

Unit 1 – Discovering Social Skills
Ways to Show Appreciation

❖

❖

❖

the
WANNA PLAY
program

Unit 1 – Discovering Social Skills
Things We Can Find Out About Friends

❖

❖

❖

the
WANNA PLAY
program

Unit 1 – Discovering Social Skills
Our Friends

❖

❖

❖

the
WANNA PLAY
program

Unit 1 – Discovering Social Skills
How Our Friends Act

❖

❖

❖

the
WANNA PLAY
program

Unit 2 – Using Appropriate Eye Contact for Interaction
Why We Look at Other People

❖

❖

❖

the
WANNA PLAY
program

Unit 2 – Using Appropriate Eye Contact for Interaction
Why Other People Look at Us

❖

❖

❖

the
WANNA PLAY
program

Unit 2 – Using Appropriate Eye Contact for Interaction
Where We Look When We Are Talking

❖

❖

❖

the
WANNA PLAY
program

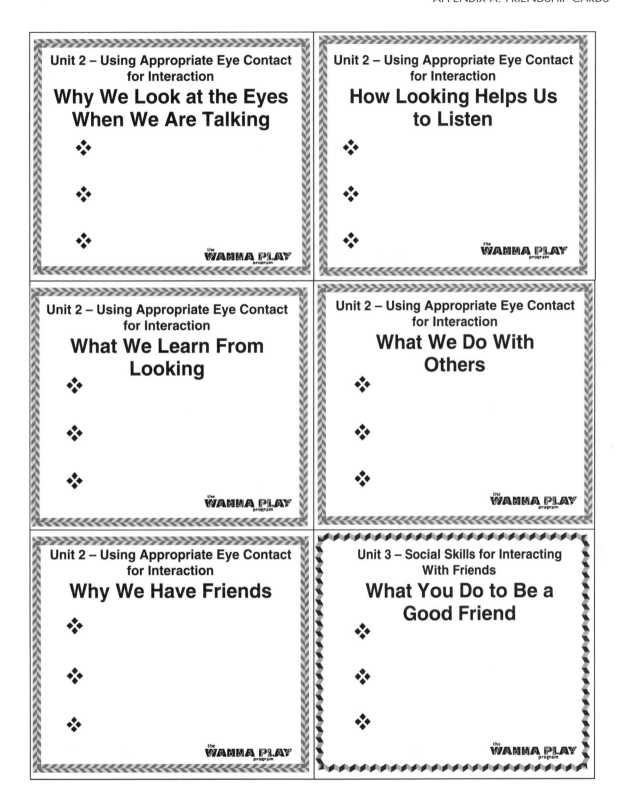

Unit 2 – Using Appropriate Eye Contact for Interaction
Why We Look at the Eyes When We Are Talking

❖

❖

❖

the WANNA PLAY program

Unit 2 – Using Appropriate Eye Contact for Interaction
How Looking Helps Us to Listen

❖

❖

❖

the WANNA PLAY program

Unit 2 – Using Appropriate Eye Contact for Interaction
What We Learn From Looking

❖

❖

❖

the WANNA PLAY program

Unit 2 – Using Appropriate Eye Contact for Interaction
What We Do With Others

❖

❖

❖

the WANNA PLAY program

Unit 2 – Using Appropriate Eye Contact for Interaction
Why We Have Friends

❖

❖

❖

the WANNA PLAY program

Unit 3 – Social Skills for Interacting With Friends
What You Do to Be a Good Friend

❖

❖

❖

the WANNA PLAY program

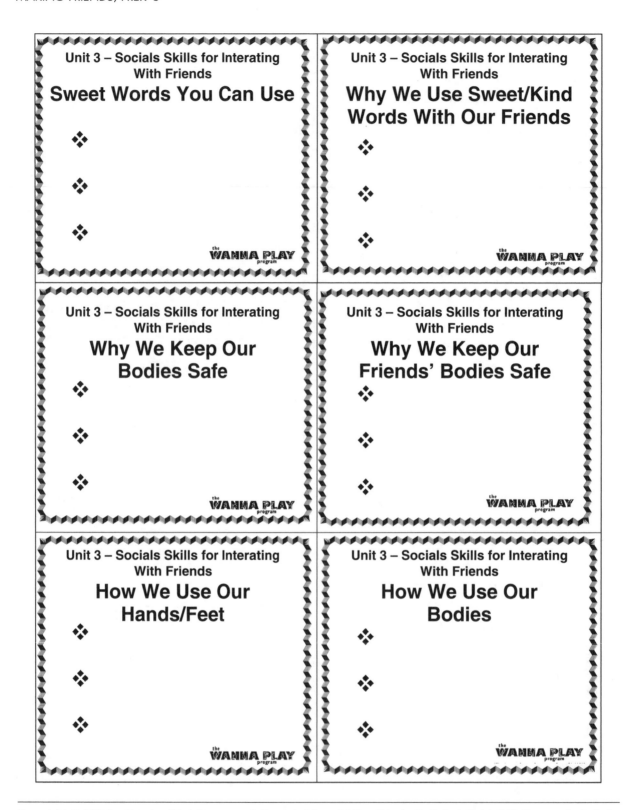

Unit 3 – Socials Skills for Interating With Friends
Sweet Words You Can Use
❖
❖
❖
the WANNA PLAY program

Unit 3 – Socials Skills for Interating With Friends
Why We Use Sweet/Kind Words With Our Friends
❖
❖
❖
the WANNA PLAY program

Unit 3 – Socials Skills for Interating With Friends
Why We Keep Our Bodies Safe
❖
❖
❖
the WANNA PLAY program

Unit 3 – Socials Skills for Interating With Friends
Why We Keep Our Friends' Bodies Safe
❖
❖
❖
the WANNA PLAY program

Unit 3 – Socials Skills for Interating With Friends
How We Use Our Hands/Feet
❖
❖
❖
the WANNA PLAY program

Unit 3 – Socials Skills for Interating With Friends
How We Use Our Bodies
❖
❖
❖
the WANNA PLAY program

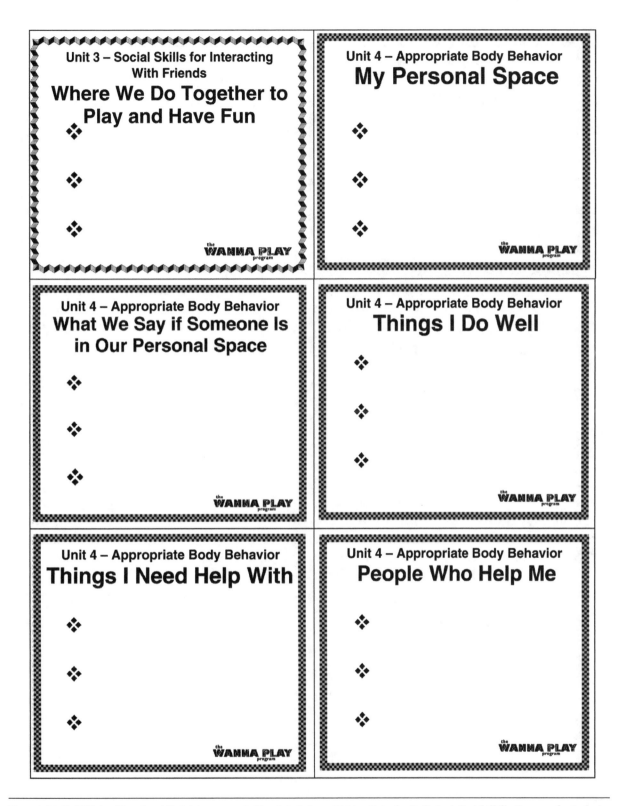

Unit 3 – Social Skills for Interacting With Friends
Where We Do Together to Play and Have Fun

❖

❖

❖

the WANNA PLAY program

Unit 4 – Appropriate Body Behavior
My Personal Space

❖

❖

❖

the WANNA PLAY program

Unit 4 – Appropriate Body Behavior
What We Say if Someone Is in Our Personal Space

❖

❖

❖

the WANNA PLAY program

Unit 4 – Appropriate Body Behavior
Things I Do Well

❖

❖

❖

the WANNA PLAY program

Unit 4 – Appropriate Body Behavior
Things I Need Help With

❖

❖

❖

the WANNA PLAY program

Unit 4 – Appropriate Body Behavior
People Who Help Me

❖

❖

❖

the WANNA PLAY program

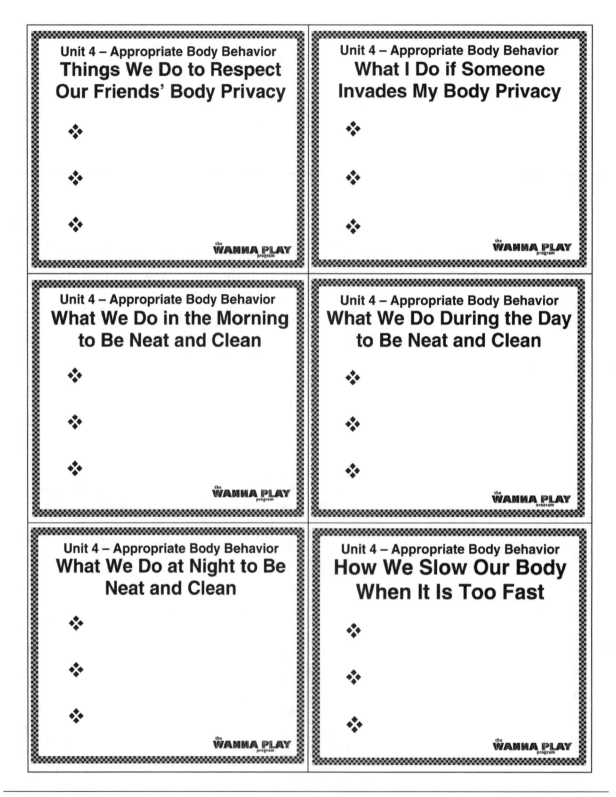

Unit 4 – Appropriate Body Behavior
Things We Do to Respect Our Friends' Body Privacy

❖

❖

❖

the WANNA PLAY program

Unit 4 – Appropriate Body Behavior
What I Do if Someone Invades My Body Privacy

❖

❖

❖

the WANNA PLAY program

Unit 4 – Appropriate Body Behavior
What We Do in the Morning to Be Neat and Clean

❖

❖

❖

the WANNA PLAY program

Unit 4 – Appropriate Body Behavior
What We Do During the Day to Be Neat and Clean

❖

❖

❖

the WANNA PLAY program

Unit 4 – Appropriate Body Behavior
What We Do at Night to Be Neat and Clean

❖

❖

❖

the WANNA PLAY program

Unit 4 – Appropriate Body Behavior
How We Slow Our Body When It Is Too Fast

❖

❖

❖

the WANNA PLAY program

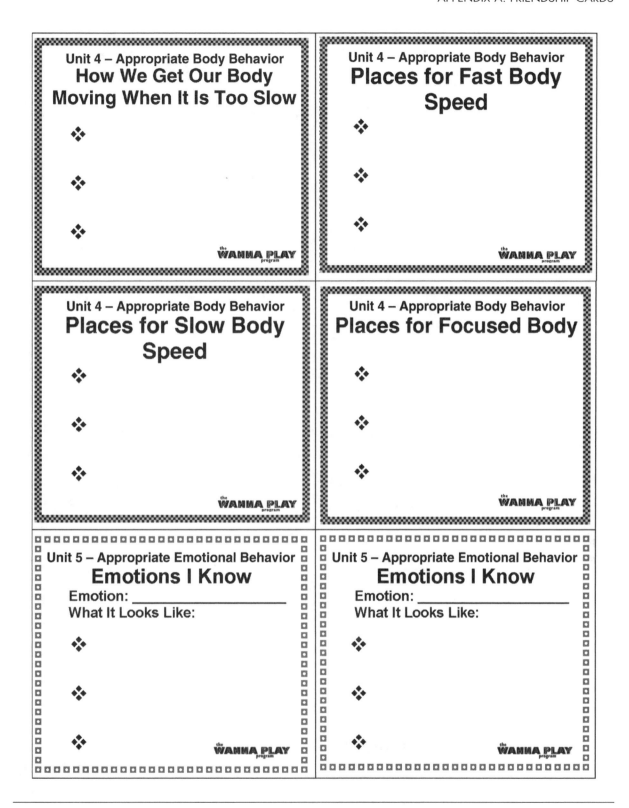

Unit 4 – Appropriate Body Behavior
How We Get Our Body Moving When It Is Too Slow

❖

❖

❖

the WANNA PLAY program

Unit 4 – Appropriate Body Behavior
Places for Fast Body Speed

❖

❖

❖

the WANNA PLAY program

Unit 4 – Appropriate Body Behavior
Places for Slow Body Speed

❖

❖

❖

the WANNA PLAY program

Unit 4 – Appropriate Body Behavior
Places for Focused Body

❖

❖

❖

the WANNA PLAY program

Unit 5 – Appropriate Emotional Behavior
Emotions I Know
Emotion: _____
What It Looks Like:

❖

❖

❖

the WANNA PLAY program

Unit 5 – Appropriate Emotional Behavior
Emotions I Know
Emotion: _____
What It Looks Like:

❖

❖

❖

the WANNA PLAY program

Unit 5 – Appropriate Emotional Behavior
Emotions I Know
Emotion: _____
What It Looks Like:

❖

❖

❖

WANNA PLAY
the program

Unit 5 – Appropriate Emotional Behavior
Emotions I Know
Emotion: _____
What It Looks Like:

❖

❖

❖

WANNA PLAY
the program

Unit 5 – Appropriate Emotional Behavior
Ways to Stay Calm

❖

❖

❖

WANNA PLAY
the program

Unit 5 – Appropriate Emotional Behavior
How to Share My Emotions

❖

❖

❖

WANNA PLAY
the program

Unit 6 – Appropriate Behavior in a Group
Interested Face

❖

❖

❖

WANNA PLAY
the program

Unit 6 – Appropriate Behavior in a Group
Listening Body

❖

❖

❖

WANNA PLAY
the program

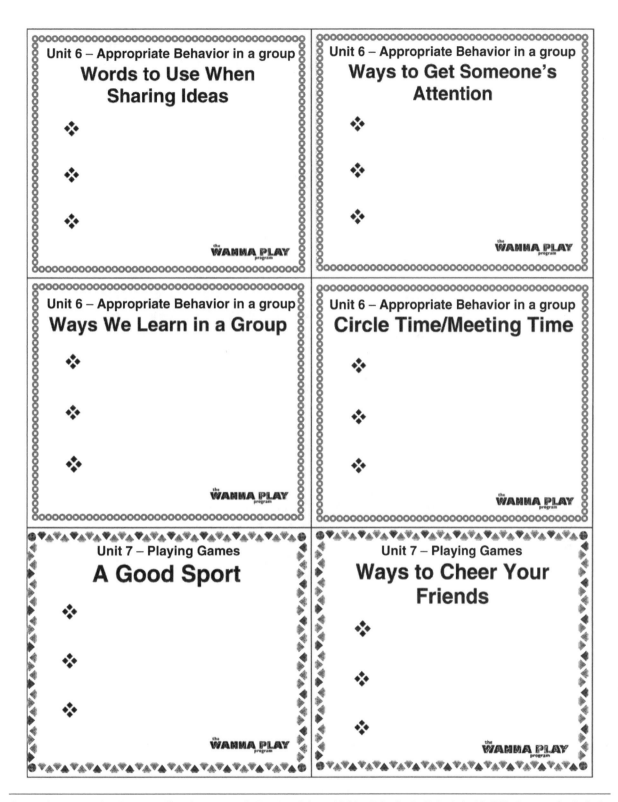

Unit 6 – Appropriate Behavior in a group
Words to Use When Sharing Ideas

❖

❖

❖

the WANNA PLAY program

Unit 6 – Appropriate Behavior in a group
Ways to Get Someone's Attention

❖

❖

❖

the WANNA PLAY program

Unit 6 – Appropriate Behavior in a group
Ways We Learn in a Group

❖

❖

❖

the WANNA PLAY program

Unit 6 – Appropriate Behavior in a group
Circle Time/Meeting Time

❖

❖

❖

the WANNA PLAY program

Unit 7 – Playing Games
A Good Sport

❖

❖

❖

the WANNA PLAY program

Unit 7 – Playing Games
Ways to Cheer Your Friends

❖

❖

❖

the WANNA PLAY program

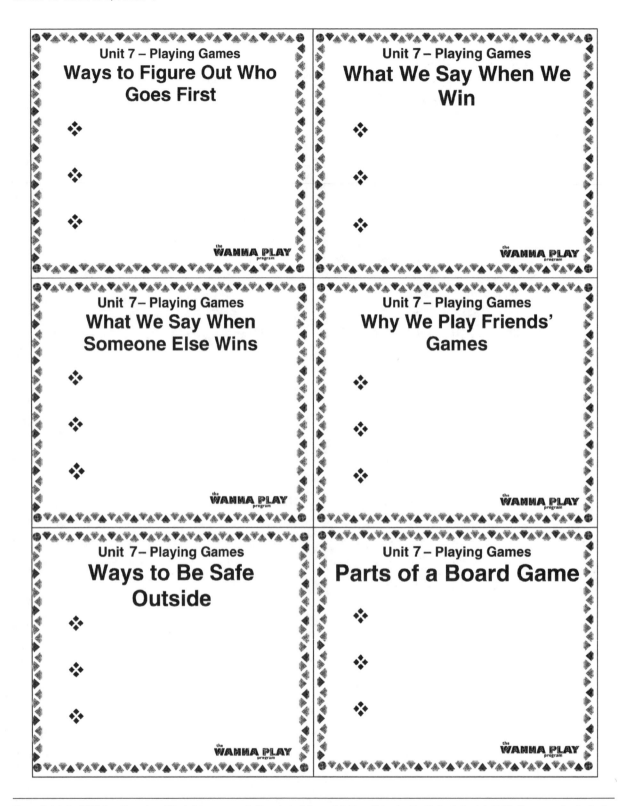

Unit 7 – Playing Games
Ways to Figure Out Who Goes First

❖

❖

❖

the WANNA PLAY program

Unit 7 – Playing Games
What We Say When We Win

❖

❖

❖

the WANNA PLAY program

Unit 7 – Playing Games
What We Say When Someone Else Wins

❖

❖

❖

the WANNA PLAY program

Unit 7 – Playing Games
Why We Play Friends' Games

❖

❖

❖

the WANNA PLAY program

Unit 7 – Playing Games
Ways to Be Safe Outside

❖

❖

❖

the WANNA PLAY program

Unit 7 – Playing Games
Parts of a Board Game

❖

❖

❖

the WANNA PLAY program

Appendix B

Worksheets and Materials

Master List

Unit 1—Discovering Social Skills

- Worksheet 1.1 Puppets for "Brown Bear"
- Worksheet 1.2 Making Friends
- Worksheet 1.3 You and Your Friend
- Worksheet 1.4 Best Friends
- Worksheet 1.5 School Friends
- Worksheet 1.6 Friend Bingo
- Worksheet 1.7 Gift of Friendship
- Worksheet 1.8 Letter to a Friend
- Worksheet 1.9 Friendship Quilt
- Picture Flashcards
- People Flashcards
- Place Flashcards

Unit 2—Using Appropriate Eye Contact for Interaction

- Worksheet 2.1 Silly Glasses
- Worksheet 2.2 Eye Coloring
- Worksheet 2.3 Who's It Going to Be?
- Social Phrases Flashcards

Unit 3—Social Skills for Interacting With Friends

- Worksheet 3.1 Friendship Train
- Worksheet 3.2 Safe Body
- Worksheet 3.3 Safe Body Clothes
- Situation Flashcards

Unit 4—Appropriate Body Behavior

- Worksheet 4.1 Appropriate Pyramid
- Worksheet 4.2 Paper Doll
- Worksheet 4.3 Paper Doll Clothes

Unit 5—Appropriate Emotional Behavior

- Worksheet 5.1 My Emotion Meter
- Emotion Bingo
- Emotion Flashcards

Unit 6—Appropriate Behavior in a Group

- Worksheet 6.1 Brainstorming for a Group Project
- Worksheet 6.2 Group Meeting Notes
- Worksheet 6.3 Group Project To-Do List
- Worksheet 6.4 Goop
- Worksheet 6.5 Interested Face
- Clue Flashcards

Unit 7—Playing Games

- Worksheet 7.1 Copy the Picture
- Worksheet 7.2 Who Goes First?
- Worksheet 7.3 Score Card A
- Worksheet 7.4 Score Card B
- Worksheet 7.5 What Happens Next?

Worksheet 1.1 Puppets for "Brown Bear"

Puppets for "Brown Bear"

Puppets for "Brown Bear" (Continued)

Puppets for "Brown Bear"

Puppets for "Brown Bear" (Continued)

Worksheet 1.2 Making Friends

Your new friend's name:

_____

Where do you see him or her?

_____

What could you say to try to make friends?

_____

_____

What are some things you could do together?

_____

_____

Why do you want to be the person's friend?

_____

_____

Worksheet 1.3
You and Your Friend

Worksheet 1.4 Best Friends

Worksheet 1.5 School Friends

Worksheet 1.6 Friend Bingo

Been to another country	Has a pet	Likes the color green	Likes to eat pizza
Has a brother or sister	Is going to the beach this summer	Likes to read	Saw/read Harry Potter
Has a Nintendo DSI	Likes to ride a bike	Shares a room with a brother or sister	Is in third grade
Likes to eat ice cream	Can blow bubbles with bubble gum	Has been to an amusement park	Can hop on one foot

Worksheet 1.7 Gift of Friendship

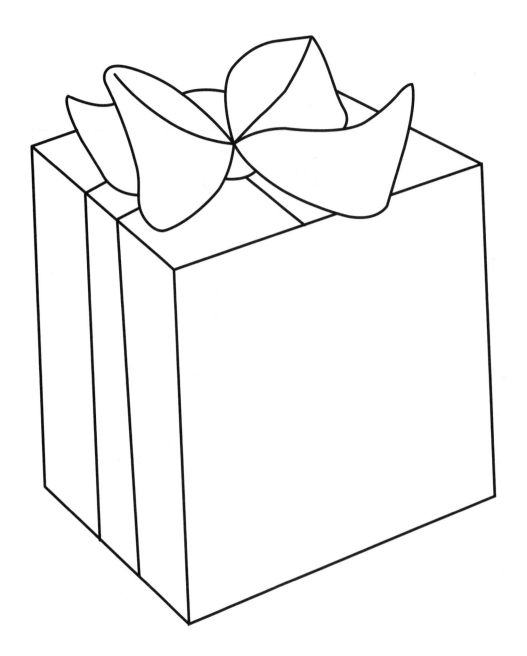

Worksheet 1.8 Letter to a Friend

Dear _____,

    I enjoyed being in your class this year.

    I really liked playing _____.

    Do you remember when we _____

_____? Would you like to play

_____ with me?

    Here is a picture of us together.

    Hope I see you soon!

    Your friend,

    _____

Worksheet 1.9
Friendship Quilt

Picture Flashcards

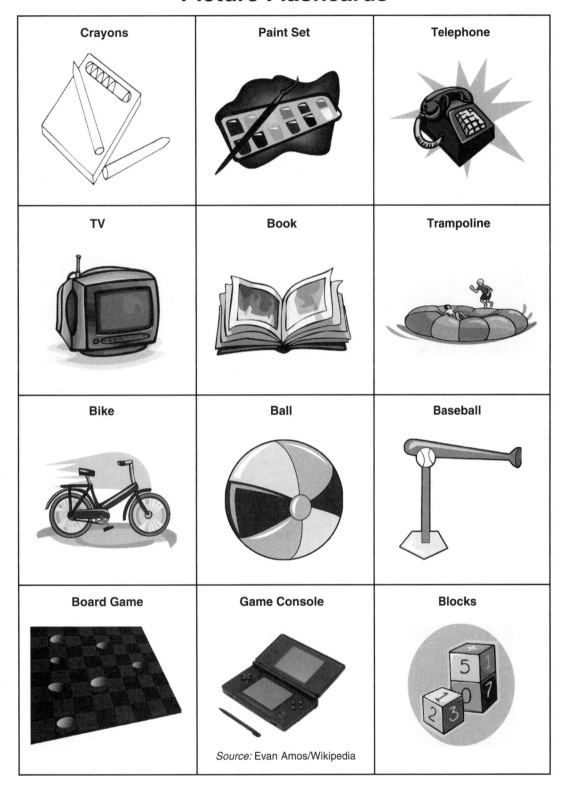

Crayons	Paint Set	Telephone
TV	**Book**	**Trampoline**
Bike	**Ball**	**Baseball**
Board Game	**Game Console**	**Blocks**

Source: Evan Amos/Wikipedia

Picture Flashcards

Sailboat	Sand Castle	Fish
Shovel and Bucket	Ladybug	Birthday Cake
Birthday Present	Pizza	Hot Dog
Ice Cream	Popcorn	Pancakes

Picture Flashcards (Continued)

Apple	Tree	Flower
Swing set	Camera	Lunchbox/Lunch Bag
Doll	Toy Car	Train
Skates	Skateboard	Guitar

Picture Flashcards

Drums	Building Blocks	Lollipop

People Flashcards

People Flashcards

Grandmother	Grandfather
Principal	Neighbor
Fire Person	Cashier at Store
Aunt	Uncle

Place Flashcards

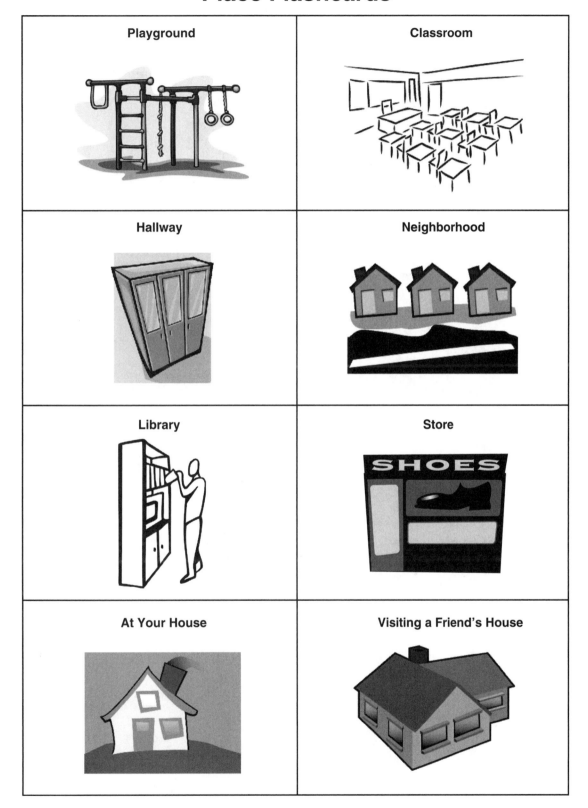

Playground	Classroom
Hallway	Neighborhood
Library	Store
At Your House	Visiting a Friend's House

Place Flashcards

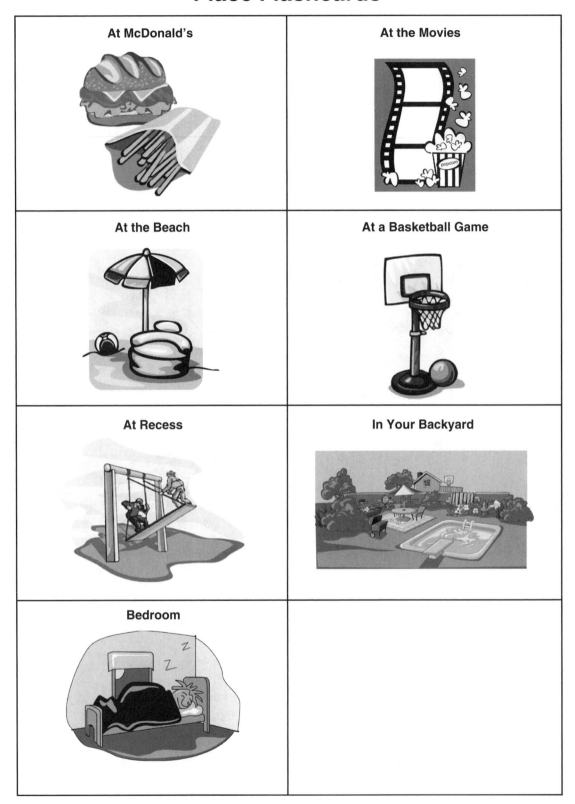

At McDonald's	At the Movies
At the Beach	At a Basketball Game
At Recess	In Your Backyard
Bedroom	

Worksheet 2.1 Silly Glasses

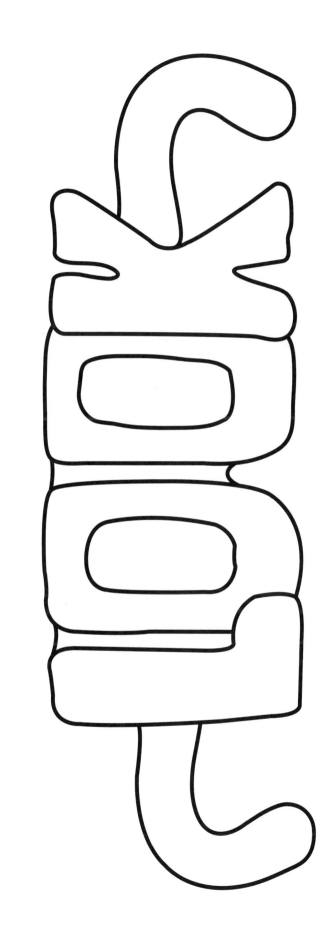

Worksheet 2.2 Eye Coloring

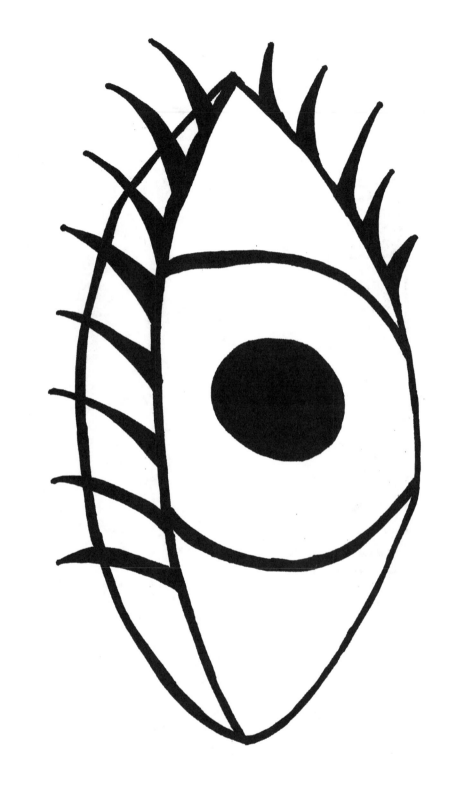

Worksheet 2.3 Who's It Going to Be?

Who do you want to . . .

sit with on the bus on a school trip? _____

be in a group project with? _____

be on a deserted island with? _____

invite over to your house? _____

go to the movies with? _____

talk about your problems with? _____

play video games with? _____

play your favorite sport with? _____

do homework with? _____

hang out at their house with? _____

eat lunch with? _____

Social Phrases Flashcards

How can I help you?	**How are you?**
Can I have that?	**Will you hand me that?**
Thank you.	**Hi!**
You're welcome.	**I'm sorry.**
I didn't mean to do that.	**Can I try again?**

Social Phrases Flashcards (Continued)

How old are you?	**God bless you.**
Excuse me.	**Do you want to come to my house?**
No thanks.	**Please wait your turn.**
Wait a minute please.	**Please leave me alone.**
Please move over.	**Please don't hit me.**

Social Phrases Flashcards

Can I have that back?	**You look nice today.**
Listen to me, please.	**I need your help.**
Good-bye.	**See you later.**
What are you doing?	**Can I go first?**
It's your turn.	

Worsheet 3.1 Friendship Train

Worksheet 3.2 Safe Body

Worksheet 3.3 Safe Body Clothes

Situation Flashcards

You are asking a friend to play.	**You are asking a teacher to help you with homework.**
You are hungry, and you want your mom to get you something to eat.	**You want a turn with a toy that your friend is playing with.**
A friend took your toy without asking.	**You want to watch TV for five more minutes when you are told to turn it off.**
A friend is talking too loudly, and you want to ask him or her to talk quieter.	**Someone hits you.**

Situation Flashcards (Continued)

You don't understand what someone has just said, and you want to ask the person to repeat it.	**There is a new student in class, and you want to say hello.**
You are playing a game with friends, and they skip your turn. Tell them that they skipped you and that you want your turn.	**You are finished playing what everyone else is playing, and you want to do something new.**
You just stepped on your friend's foot by accident.	**You want to go first.**
Your friends are playing a game, and you want to play too.	

Worksheet 4.1 Appropriate Pyramid

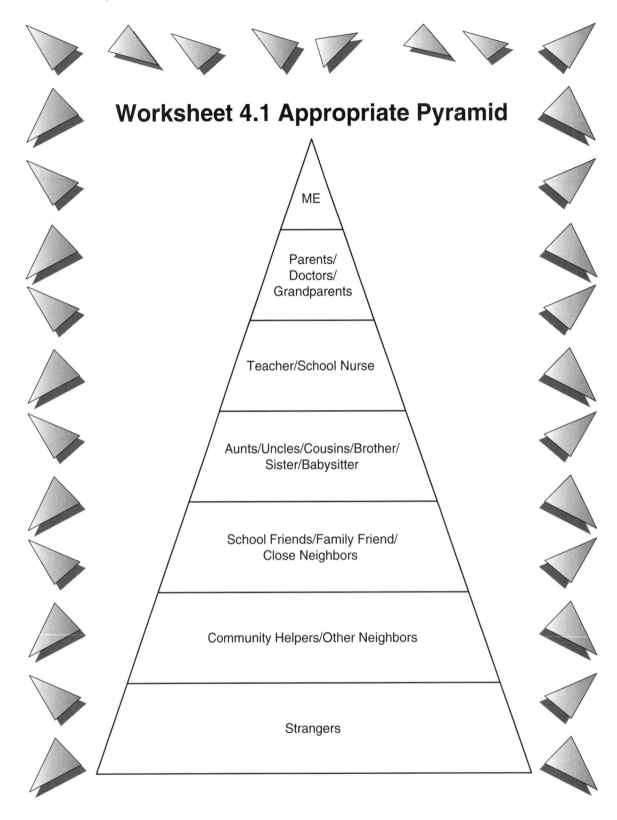

ME

Parents/
Doctors/
Grandparents

Teacher/School Nurse

Aunts/Uncles/Cousins/Brother/
Sister/Babysitter

School Friends/Family Friend/
Close Neighbors

Community Helpers/Other Neighbors

Strangers

Worksheet 4.2 Paper Doll

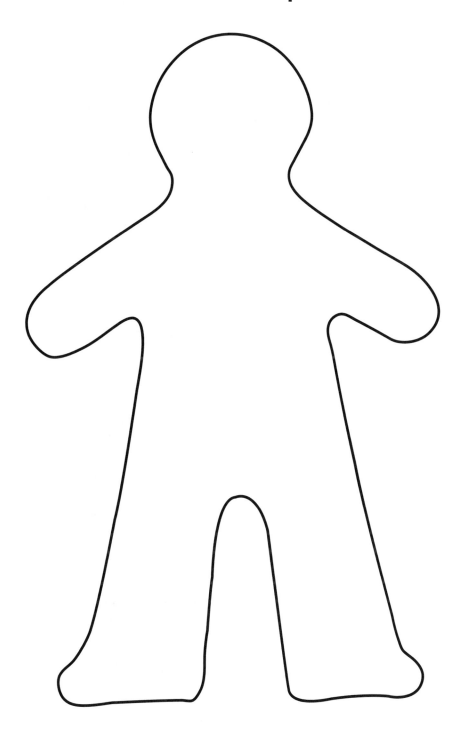

Worksheet 4.3 Paper Doll Clothes

Worksheet 5.1 My Emotion Meter

Write the emotion in the blank below. Draw the different levels of the emotion in the circles.
Rate where you are feeling in the emotion scale.

Emotion: _____

Emotion Bingo

Surprised	Sneaky	Proud
Shy	Happy	Sleepy
Confused	Silly	Talkative

Emotion Bingo (Continued)

Silly	Scared	Talkative
Mad	Happy	Curious
Enbarrassed	Nervous	Sad

Emotion Bingo

Emotion Bingo (Continued)

Calm	Surprised	Sneaky
Proud	Happy	Shy
Sleepy	Confused	Silly

Emotion Flashcards

Copy all cards and cut out. Glue on index cards for game.

HAPPY	**CALM**
SURPRISED	**SNEAKY**
PROUD	**SHY**
SLEEPY	**CONFUSED**

Emotion Flashcards (Continued)

SILLY	**SCARED**
TALKATIVE	**MAD**
CURIOUS	**EMBARRASSED**
NERVOUS	**SAD**

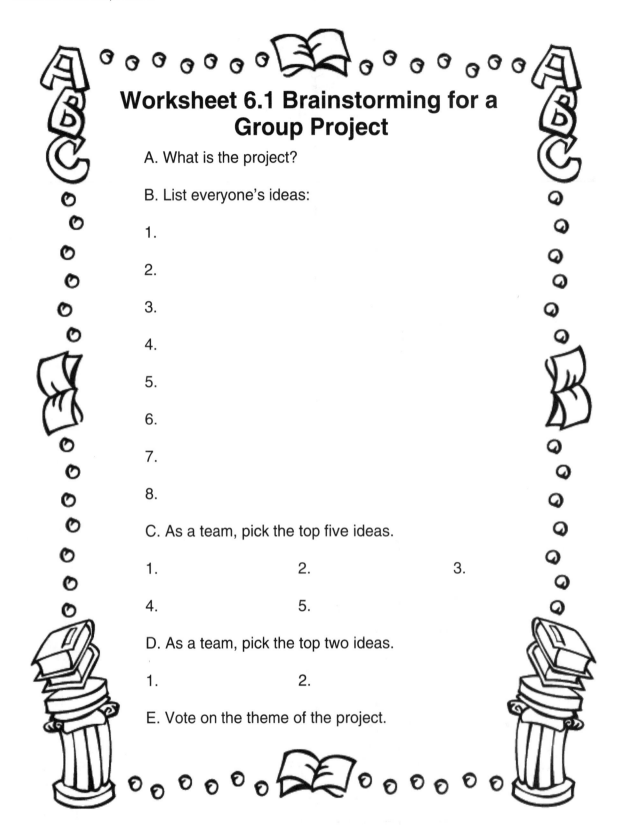

Worksheet 6.1 Brainstorming for a Group Project

A. What is the project?

B. List everyone's ideas:

1.

2.

3.

4.

5.

6.

7.

8.

C. As a team, pick the top five ideas.

1.   2.   3.

4.   5.

D. As a team, pick the top two ideas.

1.   2.

E. Vote on the theme of the project.

Worksheet 6.2 Group Meeting Notes

Date of meeting: _____

What is completed?

1.

2.

3.

4.

5.

What needs to be completed?

Who will do this? _____

Who will do this? _____

Worksheet 6.3 Group Project To-Do List

Name of project: _____

To-do list:

1.

2.

3.

4.

List each person's job:

Name:_____ 1.   Name:_____ 1.
                  2.   2.
                  3.   3.

Name:_____ 1.   Name:_____ 1.
                  2.   2.
                  3.   3.

Supplies needed: 1.

                  2.

                  3.

                  4.

Worksheet 6.4 Goop

You will need:

Cornstarch
Water
Pan
Measuring cups
Food coloring

Directions:

1. Pour one-half (1/2) cup of cornstarch in pan.

2. Fill one (1) measuring cup with water.

3. Have adult add three drops of food coloring to the cup.

4. Pour colored water into pan.

5. Use hands to mix and play with goop. ☺

Worksheet 6.5 Interested Face

Clue Flashcards

Sauce	**Brush**
Set 1	Set 2
Cheese	**Paint**
Set 1	Set 2
Dough	**Paper**
Set 1	Set 2
Pizza	**Picture**
Set 1	Set 2

Clue Flashcards (Continued)

Bubbles	Leaf
Set 3	Set 4
Can	Branch
Set 3	Set 4
Straw	Nest
Set 3	Set 4
Soda	Tree
Set 3	Set 4

Clue Flashcards

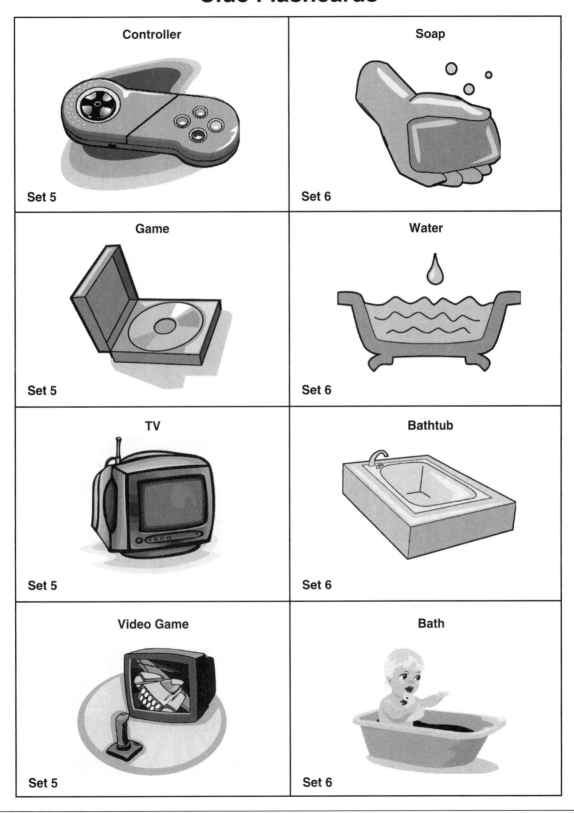

Controller	**Soap**
Set 5	Set 6
Game	**Water**
Set 5	Set 6
TV	**Bathtub**
Set 5	Set 6
Video Game	**Bath**
Set 5	Set 6

Clue Flashcards (Continued)

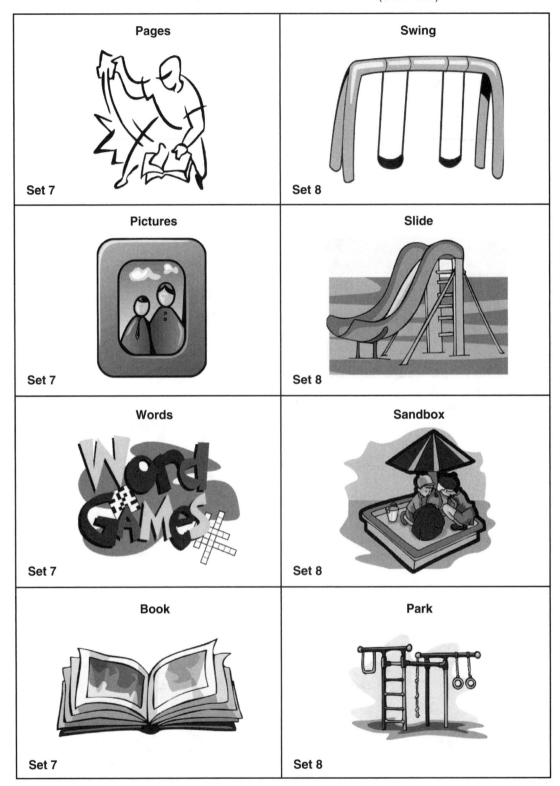

Pages	Swing
Set 7	Set 8
Pictures	Slide
Set 7	Set 8
Words	Sandbox
Set 7	Set 8
Book	Park
Set 7	Set 8

Worksheet 7.1 Copy the Picture

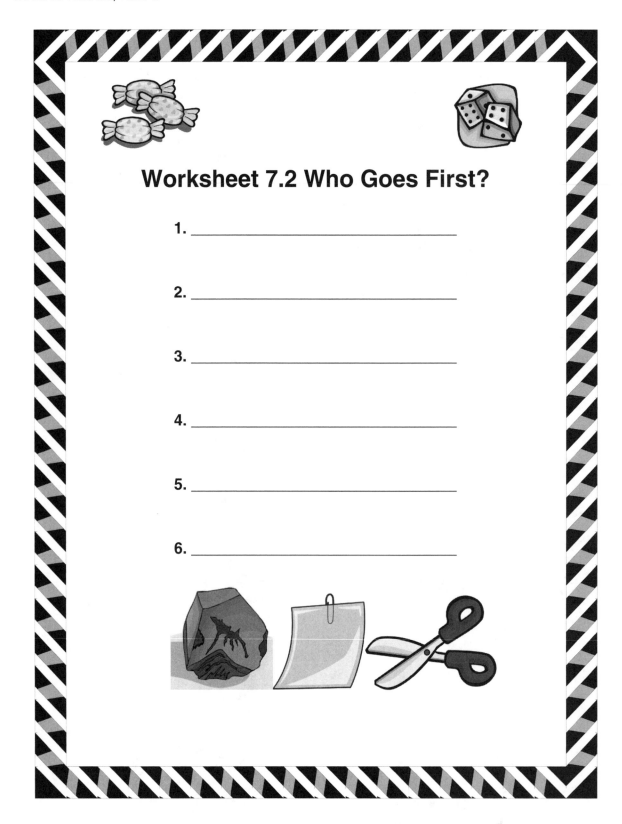

Worksheet 7.2 Who Goes First?

1. _____

2. _____

3. _____

4. _____

5. _____

6. _____

Worksheet 7.3 Scorecard A

Name	1	2	3	4

Worksheet 7.4 Scorecard B

Name	1	2	3	4	5	6	7	8	9	10

Worksheet 7.5 What Happens Next?